PENGUIN BOOKS — GREAT IDEAS

Days of Reading

Marcel Proust
1871–1922

Marcel Proust

Days of Reading

TRANSLATED BY JOHN STURROCK

PENGUIN BOOKS — GREAT IDEAS

PENGUIN BOOKS

Published by the Penguin Group
Penguin Books Ltd, 80 Strand, London WC2R ORL, England
Penguin Group (USA) Inc., 375 Hudson Street, New York, New York 10014, USA
Penguin Group (Canada), 90 Eglinton Avenue East, Suite 700, Toronto, Ontario, Canada M4P 2Y3
(a division of Pearson Penguin Canada Inc.)
Penguin Ireland, 25 St Stephen's Green, Dublin 2, Ireland (a division of Penguin Books Ltd)
Penguin Group (Australia), 250 Camberwell Road, Camberwell, Victoria 3124, Australia
(a division of Pearson Australia Group Pty Ltd)
Penguin Books India Pvt Ltd, 11 Community Centre, Panchsheel Park, New Delhi – 110 017, India
Penguin Group (NZ), 67 Apollo Drive, Rosedale, North Shore 0632, New Zealand
(a division of Pearson New Zealand Ltd)
Penguin Books (South Africa) (Pty) Ltd, 24 Sturdee Avenue, Rosebank, Johannesburg 2196, South Africa

Penguin Books Ltd, Registered Offices: 80 Strand, London WC2R ORL, England

www.penguin.com

Against Saint-Beuve and Other Essays first published 1988
This selection with some revisions and abridgements by the translator first published 2008
1

Translation copyright © John Sturrock, 1988, 2008

Set by Rowland Phototypesetting Ltd, Bury St Edmunds, Suffolk
Printed in England by Clays Ltd, St Ives plc

978-0-141-04253-4

www.greenpenguin.co.uk

Mixed Sources
Product group from well-managed
forests and other controlled sources
www.fsc.org Cert no. SA-COC-1592
© 1996 Forest Stewardship Council

Penguin Books is committed to a sustainable future
for our business, our readers and our planet.
The book in your hands is made from paper
certified by the Forest Stewardship Council.

Contents

John Ruskin

One by one, like the 'muses leaving their father Apollo to go and bring light to the world', Ruskin's ideas left the godlike head which had borne them and, embodied in living books, went to bring instruction to the nations. Ruskin had withdrawn into the solitude in which prophetic existences often end until it pleases God to call back the cenobite or ascetic whose superhuman task is done. And the mystery which was being fulfilled, the slow destruction of a perishable brain which had harboured an immortal posterity, could only be guessed at, through the veil stretched over it by pious hands.

Today death has put mankind in possession of the immense inheritance that Ruskin bequeathed to it. For the man of genius can only give birth to works which will not die by creating them in the image not of the mortal being that he is, but of the exemplum of mankind he bears within him. His thoughts are in some sense lent to him for his lifetime, of which they are the companions. On his death they return to mankind and instruct it. Such as that august family dwelling in the rue de la Rochefoucauld known as the home of Gustave Moreau while he yet lived and since his death as the Musée Gustave Moreau.

There has long been a John Ruskin Museum (in Sheffield). Its catalogue is like an epitome of all the arts and all the sciences. Photographs of paintings by the masters are found next to collections of minerals, as in Goethe's house. Like the Ruskin Museum, Ruskin's oeuvre is universal. He sought the truth, he found beauty even in chronological charts and the laws of society. But the logicians having so defined the 'Fine Arts' as to exclude mineralogy as well as political economy, it is only of that part of Ruskin's oeuvre which concerns the 'Fine Arts' as they are generally understood, of Ruskin as aesthetician and art critic, that I shall have to speak here.

It was said first of all that he was a realist. And indeed he often reiterated that the artist should apply himself to the pure imitation of nature, 'without rejecting, despising, choosing anything'.

But it has been said also that he was an intellectualist for he wrote that the best picture was the one which contained the loftiest ideas. Speaking of the group of children who are amusing themselves sailing toy boats in the foreground of Turner's 'Building of Carthage', he concludes: 'The exquisite choice of this incident, as expression of the ruling passion which was to be the source of the future greatness of the new city . . . is quite as appreciable when it is told as when it is seen, it has nothing to do with the technicalities of painting; a scratch of the pen would have conveyed the idea and spoken to the intellect as much as the elaborate realizations of colour. Such a thought as this is something far above all art; it is epic poetry of the highest order.' 'In the same way,' adds Milsand, who quotes this passage, 'when he analyses a "Holy Family" by Tintoretto, the feature by which Ruskin recognizes a great master is a ruined wall and the beginnings of some masonry, by means of which the artist gives us symbolically to understand that the birth of Christ was the end of the Jewish economy and the advent of the new alliance. A composition by the same Venetian painter, a "Crucifixion", Ruskin finds to be a masterpiece of painting because the artist has been able, by a seemingly insignificant incident, by introducing a donkey grazing off some palm leaves in the background to Calvary, to state the profound idea that it was Jewish materialism, with its expectation of a purely temporal Messiah and with the disappointment of its hopes at the entry into Jerusalem, that was the source of the hatred unleashed against the Saviour and hence of his death.'

It has been said that he did away with the role of imagination in art by giving too large a role to science. Did he not say that: '. . . every class of rock, earth and cloud, must be known by the painter, with geologic and meteorologic accuracy . . . Every geological formation has features peculiar to itself; definite lines of fracture, giving rise to fixed resultant forms of rock and earth; peculiar vegetable products, among which still further distinctions are wrought out by variations of climate and elevation . . . [The painter] observes every character of the plant's colour and form . . . he seizes on its lines of . . . rigidity or repose . . . observes its local habits, its love or fear of peculiar places, its nourishment or destruction by particular influences; he associates it in his mind with all the features of the situation it inhabits . . . He must render the delicate fissure, and descending curve, and undulating shadow of the mouldering soil with gentle and fine finger like the touch of the rain itself . . . The greatest picture is that which conveys to the mind of the spectator the greatest number of the greatest ideas.'

But it has been said in return that he ruined science by giving too large a place in it to the imagination. And indeed, one can but think of the simple-minded finalism of Bernardin de Saint-Pierre saying that God has divided melons into slices so as to make them easier for men to eat, when one reads passages such as this: '. . . God has employed colour in His creation as the unvarying accompaniment of all that is purest, most innocent, and most precious; while for things precious only in material uses, or dangerous, common colours are used . . . look at a dove's neck, and compare it with the grey back of a viper . . . So again, the crocodile and alligator are grey, but the innocent lizard green and beautiful.'

Although it has been said that he reduced art to being merely the vassal of science, since he carried his theory of the work of art seen as giving us facts about the nature of things to the point of declaring that 'a Turner discloses more about the nature of rocks than any academy will ever know,' and that 'a Tintoretto need only let his hand go to reveal a multitude of truths about the play of the muscles which will confound all of the world's anatomists,' it has been said also that he humbled science before art.

It has been said lastly that he was a pure aesthetician and that his one religion was that of Beauty, because he in fact loved it throughout his life.

But it has been said on the other hand that he was not even an artist, because into his appreciation of beauty he intruded considerations that were perhaps higher but were certainly alien to aesthetics. The first chapter of *The Seven Lamps of Architecture* lays down that the architect should use the most precious and durable materials, an obligation made to derive from the sacrifice of Jesus and the permanent conditions of that sacrifice agreeable to God, conditions we have no call to think have been modified, God not having let us know explicitly that they have been. And here is one of his arguments in *Modern Painters*, in order to settle the question of knowing who is right between the supporters of colour and the adepts of chiaroscuro: '. . . but take a wider view of nature, and compare generally rainbows, sunrises, roses, violets, butterflies, birds, gold-fish, rubies, opals, and corals, with alligators, hippopotami, . . . sharks, slugs, bones, fungi, fogs, and corrupting, stinging, destroying things in general, and you will feel then how the question stands between the colourists and the chiaroscurists, – which of them have nature and life on their side, and which have sin and death.'

And because so many contrary things have been said about Ruskin, the conclusion is that he was contradictory.

Of all these aspects of Ruskin's physiognomy, the one we are most familiar with, because it is the one of which we possess, if I may so put it, the most painstaking and successful, the most striking and widely known portrait, is the Ruskin who throughout his life knew of only one religion: that of Beauty.

It may be the literal truth that the worship of Beauty was the perpetual activity of Ruskin's life; but I adjudge that the object of that life, its deep, secret and constant intention, was other, and if I say so it is not in order to go against the system of M. de la Sizeranne, but to prevent his being depreciated in readers' minds by an interpretation which is false but natural and as if inevitable.

Not only was Ruskin's principal religion religion as such (I shall return to this point in a moment, because it dominates and characterizes his aesthetic), but to remain for the present with his 'Religion of Beauty', our own age must be warned that, if it wishes to refer truthfully to Ruskin, it cannot utter these words without emending the sense which its aesthetic dilettantism is too inclined to lend to them. In fact, for an age of dilettantes and aesthetes, a worshipper of Beauty is a man who, practising no other form of worship but his own, and acknowledging no other god but it, must spend his life in the enjoyment afforded by the voluptuous contemplation of works of art.

But, for reasons the wholly metaphysical search for which would go beyond a mere essay on art, Beauty cannot be loved in a fruitful manner if one loves it simply for the pleasures it affords. And just as to seek for happiness for its own sake leads only to tedium, and to find it one must seek for something other than it, so aesthetic pleasure is given to us in addition if we love Beauty for its own sake, as something real existing outside of ourselves and infinitely more important than the joy it affords us. Very far from being a dilettante or an aesthete, Ruskin was the precise opposite, one of those Carlyle-like men warned by their genius of the vanity of all pleasure and at the same time of the presence close beside them of a timeless reality, intuitively perceived by their inspiration. Their talent is given to them as an ability to capture this omnipotent and timeless reality, to which they dedicate, enthusiastically and as if in obedience to a command from their conscience, their fleeting lifetimes, in order to endow them with value. Such men, attentive and anxious, faced by a universe needing to be deciphered, are warned as to those elements of reality on which their special gifts will shed a peculiar light for them, by a sort of demon who guides them, of a voice that they can hear, the timeless inspiration of beings of genius. Ruskin's special gift was the sense of Beauty, in nature as in art. It was in Beauty that his temperament led him to seek for reality, and hence his wholly religious life was spent wholly aesthetically. But he did not conceive of the Beauty to which he thus found himself devoting his life as an object of enjoyment designed to attract him, but as a reality infinitely more important than life itself, for which he would have given his own life. You will see Ruskin's aesthetic follow from this. You must understand first of all that the years in which he came to know a new school of architecture or of painting may have been the principal landmarks of his moral life. He can speak of the years when the Gothic made its appearance for him with the same gravity, the same recurrence of emotion, the same serenity as a Christian speaks of the day when the truth was revealed to him. The events of his life were intellectual ones and its important landmarks those when he penetrated into a new form of art, the year when he understood Abbeville, the year when he understood Rouen, the day when the painting of Titian and the shadows in Titian's painting seemed nobler to him than the painting of Rubens and the shadows in Rubens's painting.

You must understand next that the poet being for Ruskin, as for Carlyle, a sort of scribe writing down at nature's dictation a more or less important part of her secret, the artist's first duty is to add nothing of his own pressing to this message from God. From which height the complaints of realism as well as of intellectualism directed at Ruskin can be seen to evaporate, like clouds that hug the ground. If such objections are wide of the mark, it is because they do not aim high enough. Such criticisms mistake the right altitude. The reality which the artist must record is at once material and intellectual. Matter is real because it is an expression of the mind. As for mere appearances, no one was more sardonic than Ruskin about those who see the object of art as being their imitation. 'The simple pleasure in the imitation,' he says, 'would be precisely of the same degree (if the accuracy could be equal), whether the subject of it were the hero or his horse ... we may consider tears as a result of agony or of art, whichever we please, but not of both at the same moment. If we are surprised by them as an attainment of the one, it is impossible we can be moved by them as a sign of the other.' If he attaches such importance to the way things look, this is because it alone reveals their underlying nature. M. de la Sizeranne has given us an admirable translation of a passage where Ruskin shows that the 'leading' lines of a tree can reveal to us which troublesome trees have pushed it to one side, which winds have tormented it, etc. The configuration of something is not simply the image of its nature, it is the clue to its destiny and the transcript of its history.

Another consequence of which conception of art is this: if reality is one and the man of genius he who sees it, what importance does the substance in which he represents it have, be it pictures, statues, symphonies, laws, actions? In his *Heroes and Hero-Worship* Carlyle makes no distinction between Shakespeare and Cromwell, Mohammed and Burns. Emerson numbers Swedenborg as well as Montaigne among his *Representative Men*. Where the system goes too far is, because the reality being translated is one, in not distinguishing profoundly enough between the different modes of translation. Carlyle says that it was inevitable that Boccaccio and Petrarch should have been good diplomats because they were good poets. Ruskin commits the same error when he says that 'a painting is beautiful to the extent that the ideas it translates into images are independent of the language of images.' If Ruskin's system errs in any direction, it is in this one, it seems to me. Because painting cannot attain to the unitary reality of things and hence compete with literature, except on condition that it not be literary.

If Ruskin promulgated the artist's duty as being scrupulously to obey these 'voices' of his genius which tell him what is real and to be transcribed, it was because he himself had had experience of what was genuine in inspiration, infallible in enthusiasm and fruitful in reverence. Only, although what excites enthusiasm, commands reverence and prompts inspiration be different for each one of us, we each end by attributing to it a more particularly sacred character. It can be said that for Ruskin this revelation, this guide was the Bible.

Here let us pause as at a fixed point, at the centre of gravity of Ruskin's aesthetic. Thus it was that his religious sense directed his aesthetic sense. And first, to those who may think that it adulterated it, that into the artistic appreciation of monuments, statues and pictures it introduced religious considerations which had no place there, I shall answer that it was quite the reverse. That something divine which Ruskin sensed deep inside the feeling inspired in him by works of art was precisely what was profound and original about that feeling, which imposed itself on his taste without being susceptible to modification. And the religious reverence that he brought to the expression of this feeling, his fear of subjecting it to the least distortion in translating it, prevented him, contrary to what has often been supposed, from ever introducing into his impressions of works of art any artifice of reasoning that was foreign to them. So that those who see in him a moralist or an apostle loving in art what is not art, are equally as mistaken as those who, ignoring the profound essence of his aesthetic feeling, confuse it with a sensual dilettantism. So that, finally, his religious fervour, which had been the token of his aesthetic sincerity, further reinforced it and shielded it against all interference from without. It is as I see it of no importance that this or that notion of his supernatural aesthetic should be false. All those who have some idea of the laws by which genius develops know that its strength is measured more by the strength of its beliefs than by whatever satisfaction the object of those beliefs may offer to common sense. But since Ruskin's Christianity was of the very essence of his intellectual nature, his artistic preferences, equally profound, had to have some kinship with it. And so, just as his love of Turner's landscapes corresponded in Ruskin to that love of nature which afforded him his greatest joys, so to the fundamentally Christian nature of his thought there corresponded his permanent predilection, which dominated the whole of his life, the whole of his work, for what may be called Christian art: the architecture and sculpture of the French Middle Ages, the architecture, sculpture and painting of the Italian Middle Ages. There is no need to search in his life for evidence of the disinterested passion with which he loved their works, you will find the proof of it in his books. So vast was his experience that very often the most thorough knowledge displayed in one work is neither used nor mentioned, even by way of allusion, in those other of his books where it would be appropriate. Such are his resources that he does not lend us his words; he gives them to us and does not take them back. You know, for example, that he wrote a book on Amiens cathedral. From which you might conclude that that was the cathedral he loved the most and knew the best. Yet in *The Seven Lamps of Architecture*, where Rouen cathedral is named forty times as an example, and that of Bayeux nine times, Amiens is not named once. In *Val d'Arno*, he confesses that the church that made him the most profoundly drunk on Gothic was Saint-Urbain in Troyes.

Yet, not once in *The Seven Lamps* nor in *The Bible of Amiens* is mention made of Saint-Urbain. So far as the lack of references to Amiens in *The Seven Lamps* is concerned, perhaps you imagine that he only came to know Amiens at the end of his life? Far from it. In 1859, in a lecture given in Kensington, he compares the Vierge Dorée of Amiens at length with the statues, less skilful as art but more profound in feeling, which appear to be holding up the west porch of Chartres. Yet in *The Bible of Amiens*, where one might suppose that he had brought together all his thoughts about Amiens, not once, in the pages where he speaks of the Vierge Dorée, does he make reference to the statues of Chartres. Such is the infinite wealth of his love and of his knowledge. Usually, with a writer, the harking back to certain favourite examples, or even the repetition of certain developments, reminds us that we have to deal with a man who had a certain life, particular knowledge which took the place of some other knowledge, and a limited experience from which he drew all the advantage he could. Merely by consulting the index to Ruskin's various books, the constant novelty of the works cited there, and even more the spurning or, very often, abandoning for good of an item of knowledge used only once, give one a sense of something more than human, or rather the impression that each book is by someone new, who has other knowledge, not the same experience, another life.

The delightful game he played with his inexhaustible riches was forever to be drawing new treasures out from the wonderful jewel-cases of his memory: one day the precious rose window of Amiens, another day the golden lacework of the porch at Abbeville, and to wed these to the dazzling gems of Italy.

He was able indeed to pass from one country to another in this way because the same soul that he had worshipped in the stones of Pisa was that which had also given their immortal form to the stones of Chartres. No one has had his sense of the oneness of the Christian art of the Middle Ages, from the banks of the Somme to the banks of the Arno, and he has realized in our hearts the dream of the great medieval popes for a 'Christian Europe'. If, as has been said, his name has to remain tied to Pre-Raphaelitism, we should understand by that not the one following Turner but that from before Raphael. Today we can forget the services he rendered to Hunt, to Rossetti, to Millais; but we cannot forget what he did for Giotto, for Carpaccio, for Bellini. His godlike task was not to arouse the living but to resurrect the dead.

Is this oneness of the Christian art of the Middle Ages not everywhere to be seen in the perspective of those passages in which his imagination here and there illuminates the stones of France with a magical reflection from Italy? A moment ago we saw him in *Pleasures of England* comparing the Amiens Charity with that of Giotto. In *The Nature of Gothic* see how he compares the way in which flames are treated in Italian Gothic and in French, where he takes the porch of Saint-Maclou in Rouen for his example. And in *The Seven Lamps of Architecture*, in connection with this same porch, see how something of the colours of Italy plays over its grey stones.

'The subject of the tympanum bas-relief is the Last Judgement, and the sculpture of the Inferno side is carried out with a degree of power whose fearful grotesqueness I can only describe as a mingling of the minds of Orcagna and Hogarth. The demons are perhaps even more awful than Orcagna's; and, in some of the expressions of debased humanity in its utmost despair, the English painter is at least equalled. Not less wild is the imagination which gives fury and fear even to the placing of the figures. An evil angel, poised on the wing, drives the condemned troops from before the Judgement seat . . . but they are urged by him so furiously, that they are driven not merely to the extreme limit of that scene, which the sculptor confined elsewhere within the tympanum, but out of the tympanum and into the niches of the arch; while the flames that follow them, bent by the blast, as it seems, of the angel's wings, rush into the niches also, and burst up through their tracery, the three lowermost niches being represented as all on fire, while, instead of their usual vaulted and ribbed ceiling, there is a demon in the roof of each, with his wings folded over it, grinning down out of the black shadow.'

Nor was this parallelism between the different kinds of art and different countries the most profound one he was to insist on. He was to be struck by the identity of certain religious ideas in pagan and Christian symbols. M. Ary Renan has remarked, very profoundly, how much of Christ there is in Gustave Moreau's Prometheus. Ruskin, whose devotion to Christian art never made him contemptuous of paganism, compared in an aesthetic and religious sense the lion of St Jerome with the Nemean lion, Virgil with Dante, Samson with Hercules, Theseus with the Black Prince, the prophecies of Isaiah with the prophecies of the Cumean sibyl. There is no call, certainly, to liken Ruskin to Gustave Moreau, but it can be said that a natural tendency, fostered by their acquaintance with the Primitives, led both to proscribe in art the expression of violent feelings and, in so far as it was applied to the study of symbols, to a certain fetishism in the worship of the symbols themselves, a fetishism that carried few dangers however for minds so fundamentally attached to the feeling symbolized that they could pass from one symbol to another without being detained by mere differences of surface. As for the systematic prohibition of the expression of violent emotion in art, the principle which M. Ary Renan has called the principle of Beautiful Inertia, where can we find it better defined than in the passages on 'The relation of Michaelangelo to Tintoretto'?[1] Was it not inevitable that his study of medieval French and Italian art should lead to his somewhat exclusive worship of symbols? And because he was searching, beneath the work of art, for the soul of an age, the resemblance between the symbols of the portal at Chartres and the frescoes of Pisa was bound to affect him as a proof of the originality typical of the spirit by which artists were then inspired, and their differences as evidence of its variety. With anyone else the aesthetic response might have risked being chilled by reasoning. But in him all was love, and iconography, as he understood it, might better have been called iconolatry. At this point, moreover, art criticism gives way to something greater perhaps; its procedures are those almost of science, it is a contribution to history. The appearance in the porches of cathedrals of some new quality informs us of changes no less profound in the history, not only of art but of civilization, as those announced to geologists by the appearance on earth of a new species. The stone sculpted by nature is no more instructive than the stone sculpted by the artist, and we derive no greater profit from that which preserves for us some ancient monster than that which exhibits a new god to us.

From this point of view the drawings which accompany Ruskin's writings are highly significant. In the one plate you may find a single architectural motif as treated at Lisieux, Bayeux, Verona and Padua, as if we had to do with the varieties of a single species of butterfly in different climes. But the stones which he so loved never become abstract examples for him. On each stone you can see the nuance of the passing moment joined with the colour of the centuries. '. . . Rushing down the street to see St Wulfran again,' he tells us, *'before the sun was off the towers*, are things to cherish the past for, – to the end.' He went further even; he made no separation between the cathedrals and that background of rivers and valleys against which they appear to the traveller as he approaches, like in a primitive painting. One of his most instructive drawings in this respect is that reproduced in the second engraving of 'Our Fathers have told us' entitled 'Amiens, Jour des Trépassés'. In the towns of Amiens, Abbeville, Beauvais and Rouen, consecrated by Ruskin's stay in them, he spent his time sketching, either in the churches ('without being disturbed by the sacristan') or else in the open air. And what delightful, transient colonies they must have formed in these towns, the troupe of sketchers and engravers whom he took with him, just as Plato shows us the Sophists following Protagoras from town to town, and similar also to the swallows, in imitation of which they would pause for choice on the old roofs and ancient towers of the cathedrals. Perhaps some of these disciples of Ruskin's are still to be met with who accompanied him to the banks of this re-evangelized Somme, as if the days of St Firmin and St Salve had returned, and who, while the new apostle was talking and explicating Amiens like a Bible, made instead of notes drawings, graceful notes the folder of which is doubtless to be found in some English museum room and in which I imagine reality will have been slightly rearranged, in the style of Viollet-le-Duc. The engraving 'Amiens, Jour des Trépassés' seems a little too beautiful to be true. Is it the perspective alone which, from the banks of a widened Somme, brings the cathedral and the church of St Leu so close together? Ruskin it is true might answer us back by repeating on his own account the words of Turner which he quotes in *The Eagle's Nest* and which M. de la Sizeranne has translated: '. . . Turner, in his early life, was sometimes good-natured, and would show people what he was about. He was one day making a drawing of Plymouth harbour, with some ships at the distance of a mile or two, seen against the light. Having shown this drawing to a naval officer, the naval officer observed with surprise, and objected with very justifiable indignation, that the ships of the line had no port-holes. "No," said Turner, "certainly not. If you will walk up to Mount Edgecumbe, and look at the ships against the sunset, you will find you can't see the port-holes." "Well, but," said the naval officer, still indignant, "you know the port-holes are there." "Yes," said Turner, "I know that well enough; but my business is to draw what I see, and not what I know is there."'

If, when in Amiens, you take the direction of the slaughter-house, you will get a prospect no different from that in the engraving. You will see the distance arrange, in the deceptive but happy manner of an artist, monuments which, if you then draw closer, will resume their earlier, quite different positions; you will see it, for example, inscribe the shape of one of the town's water installations on the façade of the cathedral, and create a plane out of a three-dimensional geometry. But if you nevertheless find this landscape, tastefully composed by your perspective, somewhat different from that re-counted by Ruskin's drawing, you may lay the blame above all on the changes brought about in the appearance of the town by the almost twenty years which have elapsed since Ruskin stayed there, and as he himself said of another location which he loved: 'Since I last composed, or meditated there, various improvements have taken place.'

But at least this engraving in *The Bible of Amiens* will have associated the banks of the Somme and the cathedral more closely together in your memory than your eyes no doubt could have done, no matter at what point in the town you had been placed. It will prove to you better than anything I could have said that Ruskin made no separation between the beauty of the cathedrals and the charm of the country out of which they arose, and which everyone who visits them can savour still in the particular poetry of the country and the misty or golden recollection of the afternoon he spent there. Not only is the first chapter of *The Bible of Amiens* called 'By the Rivers of Waters', but the book that Ruskin planned to write on Chartres cathedral was to be entitled. 'The Springs of Eure'. So it was not only in his drawings that he set churches on the edge of rivers and associated the grandeur of the Gothic cathedrals to the gracefulness of their French settings.[2] We would be more keenly alive to the individual charm of a landscape if we did not have at our disposal those seven-league boots which are the great expresses and were obliged, as in the old days, in order to get to some remote spot, to pass through countrysides more and more like that we are making for, like zones of graduated harmony which, by making it less easily penetrable by what is different from itself, and protecting it gently and mysteriously against brotherly resemblances, not only envelop it in nature but also prepare it in our minds.

These studies of Ruskin's of Christian art were for him like the verification and counter-proof of his ideas on Christianity and of other ideas I have been unable to indicate here but the most celebrated of which I shall allow Ruskin himself to define in a moment: his horror of machinism and of industrial art. 'All beautiful things were made when the men of the Middle Ages *believed* in the pure, joyous and beautiful lesson of Christianity.' After that he saw art as having declined along with faith, and dexterity as having taken the place of feeling. When he saw the power to realize beauty that was the privilege of the ages of faith, his belief in the goodness of faith could only grow stronger. Each volume of his last book, *Our Fathers Have Told Us* (only the first was written), was to have comprised four chapters, the last of them devoted to the masterpiece that was the fruition of the faith whose study had been the aim of the first three chapters. Thus did the Christianity that had been the cradle of Ruskin's aesthetic feeling receive its supreme consecration. And having mocked at his Protestant reader, at the moment when he led her before the statue of the Madonna, 'who must understand that neither Madonna-worship, nor Lady-worship of any sort ... ever did any human creature any harm', or before the statue of St Honoré, after lamenting that this saint was 'little talked of now in his Parisian faubourg', he might have said as at the end of *Val d'Arno*: 'And if you will fix your minds only on the conditions of human life which the Giver of it demands, "He hath showed thee, O man, what is good; and what doth the Lord require of thee, but to do justly, and to love mercy, and to walk humbly with thy God?" you will find that such obedience is always acknowledged by temporal blessing. If, turning from the manifest miseries of cruel ambition, and manifest wanderings of insolent belief, you summon to your thoughts rather the state of unrecorded multitudes, who laboured in silence, and adored in humility, as the snows of Christendom brought memory of the Birth of Christ, or her spring sunshine, of His Resurrection, you may know that the promise of the Bethlehem angels has been literally fulfilled; and will pray that your English fields, joyfully as the banks of Arno, may still dedicate their pure lilies to St Mary of the Flowers.'

Finally, Ruskin's medieval studies confirmed, together with his belief in the goodness of faith, his belief in the need for work to be free, joyous and personal, without interference from machinism. This you will best understand if I transcribe here a passage highly characteristic of Ruskin. He is talking of a small figure, a few centimetres high, lost amidst hundreds of minuscule figures, in the portal of the Booksellers in Rouen cathedral.

'. . . the fellow is vexed and puzzled in his malice; and his hand is pressed hard on his cheek bone, and the flesh of the cheek is wrinkled under the eye by the pressure. The whole, indeed, looks wretchedly coarse, when it is seen on a scale in which it is naturally compared with delicate figure etchings; but considering it as a mere filling of an interstice on the outside of a cathedral gate, and as one of more than three hundred (for in my estimate I did not include the outer pedestals), it proves very noble vitality in the art of the time . . .

'We have certain work to do for our bread, and that is to be done strenuously; other work to do for our delight, and that is to be done heartily: neither is to be done by halves and shifts, but with a will; and what is not worth this effort is not to be done at all. Perhaps all that we have to do is meant for nothing more than an exercise of the heart and of the will, and is useless in itself; but, at all events, the little use it has may well be spared if it is not worth putting our hands and our strength to. It does not become our immortality to take an ease inconsistent with its authority, nor to suffer any instruments with which it can dispense, to come between it and the things it rules: and he who would form the creations of his own mind by any other instrument than his own hand, would also, if he might, give grinding organs to Heaven's angels, to make their music easier. There is dreaming enough, and earthiness enough, and sensuality enough in human existence, without our turning the few glowing moments of it into mechanism; and since our life must at the best be but a vapour that appears for a little time and then vanishes away, let it at least appear as a cloud in the height of Heaven, not as the thick darkness that broods over the blast of the Furnace, and rolling of the Wheel.'

I will confess that rereading this passage at the time of Ruskin's death I was seized with a desire to see the little man he speaks of. And I went to Rouen as if in obedience to some testamentary thought, as if in dying Ruskin had somehow entrusted to his readers that poor creature whose life he had restored by speaking of him and who had, without knowing it, just lost for ever someone who had done as much for him as his original sculptor. But when I came close to the immense cathedral, before the door where the saints were warming themselves in the sun, higher up, from the galleries of radiant kings up to the very topmost heights of stone that I supposed to be uninhabited but where, in one place, a sculpted hermit led his isolated life, allowing the birds to dwell on his forehead, while in another a coterie of apostles was listening to the message of an angel who had settled beside them, wings folded, beneath a flock of pigeons that were opening theirs, and not far from a personage who had received a child on his back and was turning his head with a sudden, age-old gesture; when I saw, in rows before its porches or leaning from the balconies of its towers, all these stone guests of the mystical city breathing in the sunshine or the early morning shadows, I realized it would be impossible to find a figure a few centimetres high amidst this superhuman population. I went to the portal of the Booksellers none the less. But how to recognize the little figure among the hundreds of others? Suddenly a young sculptress of talent and of promise, Mme L. Yeatman, said to me: 'Here's one that looks like it.' We looked a little lower down, and . . . there it was. It wasn't ten centimetres high. It has been worn away yet its gaze is there still, the stone still has the hole picking out the pupil and lending it the expression by which I recognized it. There, amidst thousands of others, an artist dead centuries before has left this little person who dies a little each day, and who had been dead for a very long time, lost in the midst of that host of others, for ever. But he had set it there. And one day a man for whom there is no death, no infinity of matter, no oblivion, a man who, casting far away from him that annihilation which weighs us down, to pursue ends that dominated his life, so many that he was unable to achieve them all whereas we seem to lack them, this man came, and seeing, in those waves of stone where one jagged crest seemed just like another, all the laws of life, all the soul's thoughts, named them by their names, and said: 'Look, it is this, it is that.' As at the Day of Judgement, which is represented not far away, the trumpet of the archangel is to be heard in his words as he says: 'Those who have lived shall live, matter is nothing.' And indeed, like the dead represented not far away in the tympanum, who have been awoken by the archangel's trumpet and have arisen, have resumed their form, are recognizable and alive, so the little figure has come alive again and has recovered its gaze, and the Judge has said: 'Thou hast lived, thou shalt live.' He himself is not an immortal judge and his body will die; but what matter! He carries out his immortal task as if he were not going to die, unconcerned by the size of the object that occupies his time and, though having but one human life to live, he spends several days in front of one of the ten thousand figures on a church. He drew it. For him it corresponded to the ideas stirring in his brain, heedless of approaching old age. He drew it, he spoke of it. And the monstrous, inoffensive little figure was to be resurrected, against all hope, from that death which seems more absolute than others, that disappearance into the midst of an infinite number made anonymous by their resemblance, but out of which genius can quickly draw us also. Rediscovering it there, one could not but be moved. It seems to live and to be gazing, or rather to have been taken by death in the very act of gazing, like those Pompeians whose movements remain suspended. In fact it is the sculptor's idea that has been seized here in its movement by the immobility of the stone. I was touched to rediscover it there; nothing then dies of what has once lived, the sculptor's thought any more than that of Ruskin.

Coming upon it there, necessary to Ruskin, who devoted one of the very few engravings illustrating his book to it (*The Seven Lamps of Architecture*) because for him it was an actual and enduring part of his thought, and pleasing to me because his thought is necessary to me, a guide to my own which met with his along the way, I felt myself to be in a state of mind closer to that of the artists who carved the Last Judgement in the tympanum and who believed that the individual, that which is most particular in a person, in an intention, does not die but remains in the memory of God and will be resurrected. Who is right out of Hamlet and the gravedigger, when the one sees only a skull and the other recalls a fancy? Science may say: the gravedigger; but it reckons without Shakespeare, who will cause the memory of that fancy to endure beyond the dust of the skull. At the angel's summons, each one of the dead is found to be still there, in his place, when we had thought him long since turned to dust. At Ruskin's summons, we find the smallest figure, framing a tiny quatrefoil, resurrected in its form, gazing at us with the same gaze which seems to fit inside no more than a millimetre of stone. No doubt, poor little monster, I would not have been clever enough to find you, amongst the thousands of stones in our towns, to pick out your figure, to rediscover your personality, to summon you, to make you live again. Infinity, numbers, annihilation weigh us down, but it is not that they are so strong; it is that my mind is not very strong. True, there was nothing really beautiful about you. Your poor face, that I would never have noticed, does not have a very interesting expression, although obviously it has, as everyone does, an expression that no one else has ever had. But since you were sufficiently alive to continue to gaze with that same sideways gaze, for Ruskin to notice you and, after he had spoken your name, for his reader to be able to recognize you, are you sufficiently alive now, are you sufficiently loved? One can but think on you with tenderness, unkind though your look be, because you are a living creature, because, through long centuries, you were dead without hope of resurrection and because you have been resurrected. And one of these days perhaps some other person will go to seek you out in your portal, looking fondly on your oblique and spiteful face, now resurrected, because what has come from a human mind can alone one day arrest another mind which, in its turn, has fascinated our own. You were right to remain there, unregarded, crumbling away. You could hope for nothing from matter, in which you were mere nothingness. But the little ones have nothing to fear, nor do the dead. For sometimes the Spirit visits the earth; and as it passes the dead arise, and little forgotten faces recover their gaze to engage that of the living who, for their sake, abandon the living who are not alive and go to seek for life only where the Spirit has shown it to them, in stones which are already dust yet still contain human thought.

The man who enveloped the old cathedrals in more love and more joy than is bestowed on them by the sun when it adds its fugitive smile to their centuries-old beauty, cannot, if we understand him aright, have been mistaken. In the world of the spirit it is as in the universe of physics, where the height of a fountain can not exceed the height of the place from which the water has originally descended. The great beauties of literature correspond to something, and in art it is enthusiasm perhaps which is the criterion of truth. If we suppose Ruskin to have sometimes been mistaken, as a critic, in the exact assessment of a work's value, the beauty of his wrong judgement is often of greater interest than that of the work being judged and corresponds to something which may be other than it but no less precious. I do not believe that Ruskin was wrong to say of the 'Beau Dieu of Amiens' that 'no sculpture would satisfy, or ought to satisfy, the hope of any loving soul that has learned to trust in Him; but at the time, it was beyond what till then had been reached in sculptured tenderness,' and M. Huysmans right to call this same Amiens God 'a fop with a sheep's face', but it hardly matters that we should know. Whether or not the 'Beau Dieu of Amiens' is what Ruskin thought it was is of no importance for us. Just as Buffon said that 'all the intellectual beauties to be found (in a beautiful style), all the relations of which it is made up, are so many truths as useful and perhaps more precious for the public mind than those which may constitute the subject-matter,' so the truths making up the beauty of the passages in the *Bible* about the Beau Dieu of Amiens have value independently of the beauty of the statue, but Ruskin would not have found them had he spoken of it disdainfully, for enthusiasm alone could give him the power to discover them.

What it will never be given to us to know perhaps, and what in any case we cannot search for here, is just how faithfully that marvellous soul reflected the universe, and in what tempting and pathetic forms false-hood may, for all that, have insinuated itself into the very heart of his intellectual sincerity. Whatever the answer, he was one of those 'geniuses' of whom even those amongst us who were endowed at birth by the fairies have need if we are to be initiated into the knowledge and love of a new part of Beauty. Much of what is said by our contemporaries in their intellectual exchanges bears his imprint, just as on coins one sees the effigy of the reigning sovereign. In death he continues to enlighten us, like those extinguished stars whose light still reaches us, and it can be said of him what he said when Turner died: 'It is through those eyes, closed for ever in the depths of the grave, that generations yet unborn will see nature.'

'In what tempting and magnificent forms falsehood may have insinuated itself into the very heart of his intellectual sincerity . . .' This is what I meant to say: there is a sort of idolatry which no one has defined better than Ruskin himself, in a passage from the *Lectures on Art*: 'Such I conceive generally, though indeed with good arising out of it, for every great evil brings some good in its backward eddies – such I conceive to have been the deadly function of art in its ministry to what, whether in heathen or Christian lands, and whether in the pageantry of words, or colours, or fair forms, is truly, and in the deep sense, to be called idolatry – the serving with the best of our hearts and minds, some dear or sad fantasy which we have made for ourselves, while we disobey the present call of the Master, who is not dead, and who is not now fainting under His cross, but requiring us to take up ours.'

Now it certainly seems that at the basis of Ruskin's

work, at the root of his talent, one finds this very idolatry.
No doubt he never allowed it completely to overlay –
even as an embellishment, – to immobilize, paralyse and
finally to kill his intellectual and moral sincerity. In every
line he wrote, as at each moment of his life, one senses
this need for sincerity struggling against idolatry, pro-
claiming its vanity and humbling beauty before duty, be
it an unaesthetic duty. I shall not take examples of this
from his life (which was not like the lives of Racine, or
Tolstoy, or Maeterlinck, aesthetic at first and later moral,
but one in which morality established its rights from the
outset and in the very heart of his aesthetic – without
perhaps ever liberating itself as completely as in the lives
of the other Masters I have just named). I have no need
to recall its stages, for they are quite well known, from
the early scruples which he felt at drinking tea while
looking at Titians, up until the time when, having swal-
lowed up the five millions left him by his father on his
social and philanthropic work, he decided to sell his
Turners. But there is a more inward form of dilettantism
than the active form (which he had overcome) and the
real duel between his idolatry and his sincerity was
fought out not at certain moments of his life, or in certain
passages in his books, but the whole time, in those deep
and secret places, unknown almost to ourselves, where
our personality receives images from the imagination,
ideas from the intellect and words from the memory,
and affirms itself in the ceaseless choices it makes from
them and ceaselessly wagers in a sense the destiny of our
moral and spiritual lives. I have the impression that
in those places the sin of idolatry never ceased to be

committed by Ruskin. And at the very moment when he was preaching sincerity he lacked it himself, not in what he said but in the manner in which he said it. The doctrines he was professing were moral and not aesthetic doctrines, yet he chose them for their beauty. And as he did not want to present them as beautiful but as true, he was obliged to lie to himself concerning the nature of the reasons which had led him to adopt them. Hence a compromising with his conscience so unceasing that immoral doctrines sincerely professed might have been less dangerous for the integrity of his mind than these moral doctrines whose affirmation is not wholly sincere, having been dictated by an unacknowledged aesthetic preference. This sin was being committed constantly, in the actual choice of each explanation he gave of a fact, of each judgement he passed on a work, in his actual choice of the words he used – and it finally lent a mendacious attitude to the mind that was constantly giving way to it. So that the reader may be better able to judge the sort of *trompe l'oeil* which a passage from Ruskin is for anyone, including for Ruskin himself, I shall quote one of those which I find most beautiful yet where this defect is at its most flagrant. You will see that if *in theory* (in appearance, that is, the content of a writer's ideas being always the appearance, and their form the reality) beauty has been subordinated to the moral sense and to truth, in actual fact truth and the moral sense have been subordinated to the aesthetic sense, and to an aesthetic sense somewhat distorted by these perpetual compromises. The subject is 'The Causes of Venice's Decline'.

'Not in the wantonness of wealth, not in vain ministry to the desire of the eye or the pride of life, were those marbles hewn into transparent strength, and those arches arrayed in the colours of the iris. There is a message written in the dyes of them, that once was written in blood; and a sound in the echoes of their vaults, that one day shall fill the vault of heaven, – "He shall return to do judgement and justice." The strength of Venice was given her, so long as she remembered this: her destruction found her when she had forgotten this; and it found her irrevocably, because she forgot it without excuse. Never had a city a more glorious Bible. Among the nations of the North, a rude and shadowy sculpture filled their temples with confused and hardly legible imagery; but, for her, the skill and the treasures of the East had gilded every letter, and illumined every page, till the Book-Temple shone from afar off like the star of the Magi. In other cities, the meetings of the people were often in places withdrawn from religious association, subject to violence and to change; and on the grass of the dangerous rampart, and in the dust of the troubled street, there were deeds done and counsels taken, which, if we cannot justify, we may sometimes forgive. But the sins of Venice, whether in her palace or in her piazza, were done with the Bible at her right hand. The walls on which its testimony was written were separated but by a few inches of marble from those which guarded the secrets of her councils, or confined the victims of her policy. And when in her last hours she threw off all shame and all restraint, and the great square of the city became filled with the madness of the whole earth, be it remembered how much her sin was greater, because it was done in the face of the House of God, burning with the letters of His Law. Mountebank and masquer laughed their laugh and went their way; and a silence has followed them, not unforetold; for amidst them all, through century after century of gathering vanity and festering guilt, that white dome of St Mark's had uttered in the dead ear of Venice: "Know thou, that for all these things God will bring thee into judgement."

Now if Ruskin had been entirely sincere with himself he would not have thought that the crimes of the Venetians had been more inexcusable and more severely punished than those of other men because they possessed a church of multicoloured marble instead of a limestone cathedral, because the Doge's palace was next to St Mark's instead of at the other end of the town, and because in Byzantine churches, instead of being simply represented as in the sculpture of northern churches, the biblical texts of the mosaics are accompanied by lettering forming a quotation from the Gospel or the prophecies. It is none the less true that this passage from *The Stones of Venice* is of great beauty, even though it is quite difficult to account for the reasons for that beauty. It seems to me to rest on something false and I feel some scruples about yielding to it.

Yet there must be some truth in it. There is no altogether false beauty properly speaking, for aesthetic pleasure is that very pleasure which goes with the discovery of a truth. What is quite hard to say is to what order of truth the very keen aesthetic pleasure one gets from reading such a passage can correspond. It is itself mysterious, full at once of images of beauty and of religion like that same church of St Mark's, where all the figures from the Old and New Testaments appear against a background of a sort of splendid darkness and fitful brilliancy. I remember having read it for the first time in St Mark's itself, during an hour of storm and darkness when the mosaics shone with their own material light alone, with an inner, earthly and ancient gold, to which the Venetian sun, which sets even the angels of the campaniles on fire, no longer added anything of itself; the emotion which I felt on reading this passage, amidst all these angels bright against the surrounding gloom, was very strong and yet not perhaps very pure. Just as my joy grew at seeing these beautiful and mysterious figures, yet was tainted by the pleasures of erudition as it were, which I felt as I took in the texts appearing in Byzantine script beside their haloed brows, so the beauty of Ruskin's images was quickened and corrupted by the presumption of his allusions to the sacred texts. A sort of egotistical return into the self is inevitable in these joys, in which erudition mixes with art and where the aesthetic pleasures may become keener but not remain so pure. So perhaps this passage from *The Stones of Venice* was beautiful above all for affording me precisely those mixed joys I had felt in St Mark's, for it too, like the Byzantine church, had its biblical quotations inscribed beside the images in the mosaic of its style, dazzling amidst the shadows. Did the same not hold for it, more-over, as for the mosaics in St Mark's, whose purpose was to instruct and which laid no great store by their artistic beauty? Today they no longer give us anything except pleasure. Yet the pleasure their didacticism gives the scholar is a selfish one, and the most disinterested pleasure is still that given to the artist by a beauty despised by, or even unknown to those whose one purpose was to educate the people and who gave it to them as something extra.

On the last page of *The Bible of Amiens*, the 'if . . . you would care for the promise to you' is an example of the same kind. When, again in *The Bible of Amiens*, Ruskin ends the section on Egypt by saying: 'She was the Tutress of Moses and the Hostess of Christ,' we can allow the tutress of Moses: certain virtues are required in order to educate. But the fact of having been the 'hostess' of Christ may add beauty to the sentence but can it really come into the reckoning in a reasoned appreciation of the virtues of the Egyptian genius?

I have been trying to wrestle here with my most cherished aesthetic impressions, attempting to carry intellectual sincerity to its ultimate and cruellest limits. Do I need to add that if I enter this general caveat, in some sense *in the absolute*, less about Ruskin's works than about their essential inspiration and the quality of their beauty, he nevertheless remains for me one of the greatest writers of all times and all countries. Rather than seeking to decry a defect peculiar to Ruskin, I have been trying to lay hold in him, as in a 'subject' particularly favourable to such observation, of an infirmity essential to the human mind. Once the reader has understood fully in what this 'idolatry' consists, he will be able to explain to himself the excessive importance that Ruskin attaches in his essays to lettering in works of art (an importance another reason for which I indicated, far too summarily, in my preface), as well as his misuse of the words 'irreverent' or 'insolent': 'mystery which we are not required to unravel, or difficulties which we should be insolent in desiring to solve,' 'let the artist distrust the spirit of choice, it is an insolent spirit,' 'where it is just possible for an irreverent person rather to think the nave narrow than the apse high,' etc., etc. – and the state of mind which they reveal. I was thinking of this idolatry (I was thinking also of the pleasure Ruskin takes in balancing his phrases in an equilibrium which seems rather to impose a symmetrical arrangement on his thought than to receive one from it)[3] when I said: 'I do not have to look for the tempting and pathetic forms in which falsehood may have insinuated itself into the very heart of his intellectual sincerity.' But I should, on the contrary, have looked for them and I should be committing that same sin of idolatry were I to continue to shelter behind this essentially Ruskinian formula of reverence. It is not that I fail to recognize the virtues of reverence, it is the very condition of love. But where love ceases, it must never be substituted for it, so enabling us to believe without examination and to admire on trust. Ruskin moreover would have been the first to approve my not according to his writings an infallible authority, since he even refused it to the Holy Scriptures: '. . . and there is no possibility of attaching the idea of infallible truth to any form of human language . . .' But he liked the attitude of 'reverence' which believes it 'insolent to throw light on a mystery'. In order to have done with idolatry and to make yet more certain that no misunderstanding remains concerning it between myself and my reader, I would like to bring on here one of our most justly celebrated contemporaries (as unlike Ruskin in other ways as could be!) who allows this fault to show in his conversation, though not in his books, carried to such an excess that it is easier to recognize and to demonstrate it in his case, with no need any more to strive so hard to magnify it. When he talks he is afflicted – delightfully – with idolatry. Those who have once heard him will find an 'imitation' very crude in which nothing survives of his attractions, but they will know however of whom I wish to speak, whom I am taking here as my example, when I tell them that in the material in which a tragic actress is draped he recognizes admiringly the same stuff as is worn by Death in Gustave Moreau's 'The Young Man and Death', or in the costume of one of his lady friends: 'the very dress and hairstyle worn by the Princesse de Cadignan the day she saw d'Arthez for the first time.' And as he looks at the actress's drapery or at the society woman's dress he is moved by such noble associations and exclaims: 'Quite lovely!' not because the material is lovely, but because it is the material painted by Moreau or described by Balzac and hence forever sacred . . . to idolaters. In his bedroom you will find dielytras, either real ones in a vase or painted ones in a mural done by artist friends, because this is the very flower one sees represented in the Madeleine at Vézélay. As for some object that has belonged to Baudelaire, or to Michelet, or to Hugo, that he hedges about with a religious reverence. I savour too profoundly, am even carried away by, the witty improvisations into which our idolater is led and inspired by the particular kind of pleasure he finds in such veneration to wish in the very least to wrangle with him over it.

But at the very height of my enjoyment I ask myself whether this incomparable talker – and the listener who lets him go on talking – are not equally guilty of insincerity; whether because a flower (the passion flower) bears on it the instruments of the passion, it is a sacrilege to offer it to someone of another religion, or whether the fact of a house's having been lived in by Balzac (if nothing remains there anyway which might tell us something about him) makes it more beautiful. Ought we really, other than to pay her an aesthetic compliment, to prefer someone because her name is Bathilde, like the heroine of *Lucien Leuwen*?

Mme de Cadignan's costume is a ravishing invention of Balzac's because it gives us an idea of Mme de Cadignan's artistry, and informs us of the impression she wishes to make on d'Arthez and of some of her 'secrets'. But once deprived of the idea it contains, it is no more than a sign deprived of its meaning, that is to say, nothing; and to continue to worship it, to the point of going into ecstasies when one finds it again in real life on the body of a woman, that is true idolatry. This is the favourite intellectual sin of artists, to which very few of them have failed to succumb. *Felix culpa!* one is tempted to say when one sees how fruitful it has been for them in terms of charming inventions. But they should at least not succumb without a struggle. There is in nature no particular form, however beautiful, which has value except for that portion of the infinite beauty that has been able to embody itself there: not even the apple blossom, not even the blossom of the pink hawthorn. My love for these is infinite and the affliction (hay fever) which proximity to them brings on enables me each spring to give them a proof of that love not within reach of everyone. But even towards them, which are far from literary, far from being linked to any aesthetic tradition, which are not 'the actual flower to be seen in such and such a picture by Tintoret' as Ruskin would say, or such and such a drawing by Leonardo as our contemporary would say (who has revealed to us, among many other things, which everyone now speaks of yet to which no one had paid any regard before him – the drawings in the Accademia in Venice), I shall always beware of an exclusive cult that might attach itself to anything in them other than the delight they afford me, a cult in whose name, by an egotistical return into the self, I might make of them 'my' flowers and take care to honour them by decorating my bedroom with the works of art in which they appear. No, I shall not find a picture more beautiful because the artist has painted a hawthorn in the fore-ground, although I know of nothing more beautiful than the hawthorn, because I want to remain sincere and I know that a picture's beauty does not depend on the things portrayed in it. I shall not collect images of the hawthorn. I do not venerate the hawthorn, I go to see it and to breathe it in. I have allowed myself this brief incursion – which is not in any way an offensive – on to the ground of contemporary literature because it seemed to me that the features of idolatry there in germ in

Ruskin would stand out clearly to the reader when thus magnified, all the more for being so strongly differentiated. I beg our contemporary in any case, should he have recognized himself in this very clumsy pencil sketch, to believe that it was done without malice and that, as I have said, I needed to go to the furthermost limits of sincerity with myself to make this complaint against Ruskin and discover this fragile element in my absolute admiration for him. Now not only is there 'nothing at all dishonourable in sharing with Ruskin', but also I could never find any greater compliment to pay this contemporary than to have addressed the same criticism to his as to Ruskin. I can almost regret having been so discreet as not to name him. For when one is admitted into the presence of Ruskin, be it in the attitude of a donor, solely in order to hold up his book and to help it to be read more attentively, that is not a punishment but an honour.

I come back to Ruskin. So 'used' am I to him today that to grasp the evidences, and study the nature of this idolatry, and the slight factitiousness it sometimes adds to the keenest literary pleasures that he affords us, I need to descend deep into my own self. But it must often have shocked me when I was starting to love his books, before gradually closing my eyes to their defects, as happens in any love-affair. Love-affairs with living people may sometimes have a sordid origin which is later purified. A man makes the acquaintance of a woman because she can help him to achieve an end unconnected with herself. Then, once he knows her, he loves her for herself, and unhesitatingly sacrifices to her that end she was merely to have helped him to attain. Thus originally there was something self-interested mixed in with my love for Ruskin's books, a delight in the intellectual profit I was to derive from them. The fact is that, sensing the power and attraction of the very first pages I read, I made an effort not to resist them, not to argue too much with myself, because I felt that if one day the attraction of Ruskin's thought should extend for me over everything he had touched, in short if I became completely enamoured of his thought, the world would be enriched by everything of which I had hitherto been ignorant, by Gothic cathedrals and by any number of pictures in England and in Italy which had not yet awoken in me that desire without which there is never true knowledge. For Ruskin's thought is not like the thought of an Emerson, for example, which is contained in its entirety in a book, something abstract that is, a pure sign of itself. The object to which a thought like Ruskin's is applied and from which it is inseparable, is not immaterial, it is scattered across the surface of the earth. One must go to seek it wherever it is to be found, to Pisa, to Florence, to Venice, to the National Gallery, to Rouen, to Amiens, into the mountains of Switzerland. Such a thought, which has an object other than itself, which has realized itself in space, which is thought no longer infinite and free but limited and subjugated, which is incarnate in bodies of sculpted marble, in snow-covered mountains, in painted faces, is perhaps less godlike than pure thought. But it makes the universe more beautiful for us, or at least certain parts of it, certain named parts, because it has touched them and initiated us into them by forcing us, if we would understand them, to love them.

And so indeed it was; the universe suddenly took on for me again an infinite value. And my admiration for Ruskin lent to the things which he had brought me to love so great an importance that they seemed to me charged with a value higher than that of life itself. This was literally so on an occasion when I believed that my days were numbered; I set off for Venice in order, before I died, to approach, to touch, to see embodied, in palaces that were decaying yet still upright, still pink, Ruskin's ideas on the domestic architecture of the Middle Ages. What importance, what reality can a town so special, so localized in time and so particularized in space as Venice have in the eyes of someone about to take leave of the earth, and how could the theories of domestic architecture that I might study there and verify from living examples, be amongst those 'truths which dominate death, which keep us from fearing it and cause us almost to love it' (Renan)? The power of genius is to make us love a beauty we feel to be more real than ourselves, in those things which in the eyes of others are as particular and as perishable as ourselves.

The poet's 'I shall say they are beautiful once your eyes have said so' is not very true, if the eyes in question are those of the beloved. In a certain sense and whatever splendid compensations, on this same ground of poetry, it may be preparing for us, love depoeticizes nature. To the man in love the earth is nothing more than 'the carpet for the lovely child's feet' of his mistress, nature nothing more than 'her temple'. That love which uncovers so many profound psychological truths for us, excludes us on the other hand from the poetic feeling for nature, because it puts us into selfish frames of mind (love is at the highest point along the scale of selfishness, but it is still selfish) in which the poetic feeling occurs only with difficulty. Admiration for someone's thought, on the contrary, causes beauty to arise at every step because it is constantly awakening the desire for it. The mediocre usually imagine that to let ourselves be guided by the books we admire robs our faculty of judgement of part of its independence. 'What can it matter to you what Ruskin feels: feel for yourself.' Such a view rests on a psychological error which will be discounted by all those who have thus accepted a spiritual discipline and feel thereby that their power of understanding and of feeling is infinitely enhanced, and their critical sense never paralysed. Then we are simply in a state of grace in which all our faculties, our critical sense as much as the others, are enhanced. And so this voluntary servitude is the beginning of freedom. There is no better way of coming to be aware of what feels oneself than by trying to recreate in oneself what a master has felt. In this profound effort it is our thought itself that we bring out into the light, together with his. We are free in life but only if we have an aim: the sophism of an indifferent freedom was exposed long ago. Those writers who are forever emptying their minds, thinking to rid them of all outside influence so as to be quite sure of remaining personal, are obeying, unknowingly, a sophism equally as naïve. In point of fact, the only occasions when we can truly call on the full power of our minds are those when we do not believe we are acting independently, when we do not choose an arbitrary objective for our endeavours. The theme of the novelist, the vision of the poet, the truth of the philosopher, impose themselves on them in an almost necessary way, externally to their minds so to speak. And it is by submitting his mind to the conveying of that vision, to the approximation to that truth, that the artist becomes truly himself.

But in speaking of the passion, somewhat artificial to start with but later so very profound, which I had for Ruskin's thought, I speak by the light of memory and of a memory which recalls only the facts 'but can repossess nothing of the deep past'. It is only when certain periods of our lives are forever closed, when, even at those times when we seem to have been granted the power and the freedom, we are forbidden to reopen the doors to them by stealth, when we are incapable of reverting even for an instant to the state in which we were for so long, only then do we refuse to accept that such things should have been entirely abolished. We can no longer sing of them, having failed to heed Goethe's wise admonition, that there is no poetry but in the things one can still feel. But if we are unable to relight the fires of the past, we would like at least to gather up their ashes. For want of a resurrection of which we are no longer capable, we would like at least, with the frozen memory we have preserved of these things – the memory of the facts which tells us: 'you were this or that' without enabling us to become it again, which affirms the reality of a paradise lost instead of restoring it to us in memory, – to describe it and to constitute the knowledge of it. It is

43

when Ruskin is far away from us that we translate his books and try to capture the characteristics of his thought in a close likeness. And so it is not the accents of our faith or of our love that you will come to know, but our piety alone that you will perceive here and there, stealthy and impassive, busied, like the Theban virgin, on the restoration of a tomb.

Notes

1. Similarly in *Val d'Arno*, the lion of St Mark is the direct descendant of the lion of Nemea, and its plumed crest is the one to be seen on the head of the Hercules of Camarina, with the difference pointed out elsewhere in the same book 'that Herakles kills the beast and makes a helmet and cloak of its skin; the Greek St Mark converts the beast and makes an evangelist of him.' [*Val d'Arno*, 8, cciii.]

    It is not in order to find another sacred lineage for the lion of Nemea that I have quoted this passage, but to emphasize the whole idea of the end of this chapter in *The Bible of Amiens*, 'that there is a Sacred classical art'. Ruskin did not want (*Val d'Arno*) Greek to be contrasted with Christian but with the Gothic, 'because St Mark is Greek like Herakles'. We touch here on one of Ruskin's most important ideas, or more accurately on one of the most original sentiments he brought to the contemplation and study of Greek and Christian works of art, to convey which fully it is necessary to quote a passage from *St Mark's Rest* which is, in my opinion, one of those where there emerges the most clearly anywhere in Ruskin, where that particular attitude of mind can most easily be

seen at work which led him to pay no heed to the advent
of Christianity, to recognize a Christian beauty already in
the works of paganism and to trace the persistence of a
Hellenic ideal into the works of the Middle Ages. It is
quite certain that this attitude of mind, wholly aesthetic
in my view, at least logically in its essence if not chrono-
logically in its origins, became systematized in Ruskin's
mind and that he extended it into his historical and
religious criticism. But even when Ruskin is comparing
Greek royalty with Frankish (*Val d'Arno*, chapter on 'Fran-
chise'), or when he is declaring in *The Bible of Amiens* that
'Christianity brought no great alteration to the ideal of
virtue and of human happiness,' or when he speaks as we
have seen on the preceding page of the religion of Horace,
all he is doing is to draw theoretical conclusions from
the aesthetic pleasures he had felt on rediscovering a
canephoros in a Herodias, a Harpy in a cherub, a Greek
vase in a Byzantine dome. Here is the passage in *St Mark's
Rest*: 'And this is true, not of Byzantine art only, but of all
Greek art . . . Let us leave, today . . . the word "Byzantine". There is but one Greek school, from Homer's day
down to the Doge Selvo's; and these St Mark's mosaics
are as truly wrought in the power of Daedalus, with the
Greek constructive instinct . . . as ever chest of Cypselus
or shaft of Erectheum.'

Then Ruskin enters the baptistery of St Mark's and
says: 'Over the door is Herod's feast. Herodias's daughter
dances with John the Baptist's head in the charger, on her
head, – simply the translation of any Greek maid on a
Greek vase, bearing a pitcher of water on her head . . .
Pass on now into the further chapel under the darker
dome. Darker, and very dark; – to my old eyes scarcely
decipherable, to yours, if young and bright, it should be

beautiful, for it is indeed the origin of all those golden-domed backgrounds of Bellini, and Cima, and Carpaccio; itself a Greek vase, but with new Gods. That ten-winged cherub in the recess of it, behind the altar, has written on the circle on its breast, "Fulness of Wisdom". It is the type of the Breath of the Spirit. But it was once a Greek Harpy, and its wasted limbs remain scarcely yet clothed with flesh from the claws of birds that they were ... Above, Christ himself ascends, borne in a whirlwind of angels; and, as the vaults of Bellini and Carpaccio are only the amplification of the Harpy vault, so the Paradise of Tintoret is only the final fulfilment of the thought in this narrow cupola ... there is no question but that these mosaics are not earlier than the thirteenth century. And yet they are still absolutely Greek in all modes of thought and forms of tradition. The Fountains of fire and water are merely forms of the Chimera and the Peirene; and the maid dancing, though a princess of the thirteenth century in sleeves of ermine, is yet the phantom of some sweet water-carrier from an Arcadian spring.' [*St Mark's Rest, 92, et seq.* The quotations are not continuous.] Cf., when Ruskin says: 'I am alone, as I believe, in thinking still with Herodotus.' Anyone of a mind sufficiently discerning to be struck by the features characteristic of a writer's physiognomy, and who does not hold where Ruskin is concerned to everything he may have been told, that he was a prophet, a seer, a Protestant and other things which mean very little, will feel that such features, though certainly secondary, are yet very 'Ruskinian'. Ruskin lives in a sort of brotherhood with all the great minds of every age, and since he is interested in them only to the extent that they are able to answer the eternal questions, for him there are no ancients or moderns and he can talk of Herodotus as he would of a contemporary. As the ancients have no value for him except in so far as they are 'of the present day', and can serve as illustrations for our daily meditations, he does not treat them at all as ancients. And so all those of their words which have not been rejected as obsolete and are no longer seen as relating to a given epoch, have a greater importance for him, and preserve in some sense the scientific value they may once have had but of which time had deprived them. From the manner in which Horace speaks of the spring of Bandusia, Ruskin deduces that he was pious, 'in Milton's fashion'. And even at the age of eleven, learning the odes of Anacreon for pleasure, he learnt from them 'with certainty, what in later study of Greek art it proved extremely advantageous to me to know, that the Greeks liked doves, swallows, and roses just as well as I did.' [*Praeterita*, lxxxi.] Obviously for an Emerson 'culture' has the same value. But without even pausing over the differences, which are profound, let us note first of all, to stress those features peculiar to the physiognomy of Ruskin, that because he saw no distinction between science and art he speaks of the ancients as scientists with the same reverence as of the ancients as artists. When it comes to discoveries in natural history he invokes the 104th psalm, falls in with the view of Herodotus (readily opposing it to the opinion of a contemporary scientist) on a question of religious history, and admires one of Carpaccio's paintings as an important contribution to the descriptive history of parrots (*St Mark's Rest*: 'The Shrine of the Slaves'). Obviously we should soon join up again here with the idea of a classical sacred art, 'there is only one Greek art, St Jerome and Herakles, etc.', each one of these ideas leading to the rest. But for the time being we still only have a Ruskin deeply attached to his library, making no distinction between science and art, believing in consequence that a scientific theory may remain true just as a work of art may remain beautiful (this idea he never expresses explicitly, but secretly it governs all the others and alone can have made them possible), and going to an ode from antiquity or a medieval bas-relief for facts of natural history or of critical philosophy, convinced that all the sages from every age and every country are better worth consulting than the fools, be they contemporary. This inclination is of course held in check by a critical sense so right that we can have full confidence in him, and he exaggerates it only for the pleasure of making little jokes about 'thirteenth-century entomology' etc., etc.

2. What an interesting collection might be made of French landscapes as seen through English eyes: the rivers of France by Turner; Bonington's 'Versailles'; Walter Pater's 'Auxerre' or 'Valenciennes', 'Vézélay' or 'Amiens'; Stevenson's 'Fontainebleau'; and how many more!

3. I do not have the time today to make myself clear concerning this failing, but I fancy that through my translation, however flat it may be, the reader may be able to see, as through the thick but abruptly illuminated glass of a fish-tank, the rapid but perceptible snatching away of the thought by the phrase, and the instant wasting which the thought suffers.

Days of Reading (I)

There are no days of my childhood which I lived so fully perhaps as those I thought I had left behind without living them, those I spent with a favourite book. Everything which, it seemed, filled them for others, but which I pushed aside as a vulgar impediment to a heavenly pleasure: the game for which a friend came to fetch me at the most interesting passage, the troublesome bee or shaft of sunlight which forced me to look up from the page or to change my position, the provisions for tea which I had been made to bring and which I had left beside me on the seat, untouched, while, above my head, the sun was declining in strength in the blue sky, the dinner for which I had had to return home and during which my one thought was to go upstairs straight away afterwards, and finish the rest of the chapter: reading should have prevented me from seeing all this as anything except importunity, but, on the contrary, so sweet is the memory it engraved in me (and so much more precious in my present estimation than what I then read so lovingly) that if still, today, I chance to leaf through these books from the past, it is simply as the only calendars I have preserved of those bygone days, and in the hope of finding reflected in their pages the houses and the ponds which no longer exist.

Who cannot recall, as I can, the reading they did in

the holidays, which one would conceal successively in all those hours of the day peaceful and inviolable enough to be able to afford it refuge. In the mornings, after returning from the park, when everyone had gone out for a walk, I would slip into the dining-room, where no one would be coming until the still distant hour for lunch except for the old, relatively silent Félicie, and where I would have for my sole companions, most respectful of reading, the painted plates hanging on the wall, the calendar from which the previous day's page had been newly torn, the clock and the fire, which speak but without demanding that one answer them and whose quiet remarks are void of meaning and do not, unlike human speech, substitute a different meaning for that of the words you are reading. I would settle myself on a chair, near the small log fire of which, during lunch, my early rising uncle, the gardener, would say: 'That doesn't do any harm! I can put up with a bit of fire; it was jolly cold in the vegetable garden at six o'clock I can assure you. And to think it's only a week to Easter!' Before lunch, which would, alas, put a stop to my reading, lay two whole hours. From time to time one heard the sound of the pump, from which the water was about to flow, causing one to look up and gaze at it through the closed window, close by on the little garden's solitary path that edged its beds of pansies with bricks and half-moons of pottery: pansies gathered so it seemed in those too beautiful skies, those versicoloured skies that were as if reflected from the stained-glass of the church sometimes to be seen between the roofs of the village, the sad skies that appeared before a storm, or afterwards, too late, when the day was about to end. Unfortunately, the cook would come in well ahead of time to set the table; if only she had set it without speaking! But she felt it her duty to say: 'You're not comfortable like that; supposing I move the table nearer?' And merely to reply: 'No, thank you,' one had to stop one's voice dead and bring it back from far away, that voice which, inside one's lips, had been noiselessly repeating, fluently, all the words one's eyes had been reading; one had to stop it, to bring it out, and, in order to say an appropriate 'No, thank you,' to give it a semblance of ordinary life, the intonation of a reply, which it had lost. Time was passing; often there would start to arrive in the dining-room, long before lunch, those who had felt tired and had cut short their walk, had 'taken the Méréglise way' or those who had not gone out that morning, having some 'writing to do'. They would say, admittedly: 'I don't want to disturb you,' but would at once start to approach the fire, to look at the time, to declare that lunch would not be unwelcome. Whoever had 'stayed in to write' was met with a particular deference and they would say to him or her: 'You've been keeping up your little correspondence' with a smile into which there entered respect, mystery, ribaldry and circumspection, as if this 'little correspondence' were at once a state secret, a prerogative, an amorous liaison and an indisposition. Some could wait no longer and would take their places at the table, ahead of time. This was heartbreaking because it would set a bad example to the other arrivals, would make them think it was already midday and bring from my parents all too soon the fatal words: 'Come on, close your book, we're going to have lunch.' Everything was ready, the places were fully laid on the table-cloth, where all that was missing was what was only brought in at the end of the meal, the glass device in which my uncle, the horticulturalist and cook, himself made the coffee at the table, tubular and complicated like some piece of physics apparatus that smelt good and in which it was most agreeable to watch the sudden ebullition rise into the glass dome and then leave its fragrant brown ash on the steamed-up sides; as well as the cream and the strawberries which this same uncle would mix, always in identical proportions, stopping precisely at the pink colour that he required, with the experience of a colourist and the instinctive foresight of a gourmand. How long lunch seemed to last! My great-aunt did no more than sample the dishes so as to give her opinion with a quietness which would tolerate but not admit contradiction. Over a novel, or a poem, things she was an expert in, she always deferred, with a woman's humility, to the opinion of those more competent. She believed that to be the fluctuating domain of caprice in which the preference of an individual is unable to establish the truth. But over things the rules and principles of which had been taught her by her mother, the way of cooking certain dishes, of playing Beethoven sonatas, or of entertaining graciously, she was sure she knew what a proper perfection was and could tell how close or not others had come to it. In these three things, what is more, perfection was almost the same: a sort of simplicity of means, of sobriety and of charm. She rejected with horror the addition of seasonings to dishes that did not absolutely require them, that one should play affectedly or with too much pedal, that when 'entertaining' one should be other than perfectly natural or talk overmuch about oneself. From the very first mouthful, the first notes, a simple invitation, she would claim to know whether she had to deal with a good cook, a genuine musician, a woman who had been well brought up. 'She may have many more fingers than I do, but she has no taste to play that very simple andante with so much emphasis.' 'She may be a very brilliant woman full of good qualities, but it is wanting in tact to talk about oneself in such circumstances.' 'She may be a very knowledgeable cook, but she doesn't know how to do a *bifteck aux pommes*.' A *bifteck aux pommes*, the ideal competition piece, difficult by its very simplicity, a sort of Pathetic Sonata of cooking, a gastronomic equivalent of, in social life, the visit of the lady who has come to ask you to tell her about a servant yet who, in this simple act, is able to display, or to lack, so much tact and education. Such was my grandfather's *amour propre* that he would have liked all the dishes to be a success, but so ill-informed was he about cooking that he never knew when they had failed. He was quite willing to admit on occasions that they had, but very rarely and only on purely accidental grounds. My great-aunt's always justified criticisms, implying on the contrary that the cook had not known how to make a certain dish, could not fail to seem especially intolerable to my grandfather. Often, to avoid arguing with him, my great-aunt, after merely brushing it with her lips, would then withhold her opinion, which at once let us know that it was unfavourable. She remained silent, but in her kindly eyes we could read an unshakeable and meditated disapproval, which had the gift of driving my grandfather into a fury. He would beg her ironically to give her opinion, grow impatient at her silence, press her with questions, lose his temper, but one sensed that she would have accepted martyrdom rather than be made to confess what my grandfather believed: that the dessert had not been over-sweetened.

After lunch, my reading resumed straight away; especially if the day was at all warm, everyone withdrew upstairs into their bedrooms, which enabled me at once to gain my own, up the little flight of close-set stairs, on the solitary upper storey, so low that once astride the windowsill a child might have jumped down into the street. I would go to close my window without having been able to escape the greeting of the gunsmith opposite who, on the pretext of lowering his awnings, came every day after lunch to smoke his pipe in front of his doorway and to say good-afternoon to the passers-by, who would sometimes stop to converse. The theories of William Morris, applied so consistently by Maple and the English interior designers, decree that a bedroom is beautiful solely on condition that it contain only objects that are useful to us and that any useful object, be it a simple nail, should be not concealed but showing. Above the slatted and completely uncovered brass bedstead, on the bare walls of these hygienic bedrooms, a few reproductions of masterpieces. Judged by the principles of which aesthetic, my own bedroom was in no way beautiful, for it was full of objects that could serve no purpose and which modestly concealed, to the extent of making it extremely hard to use them, those which did serve a purpose. But for me it was from these very objects which were not there for my convenience, but seemed to have come for their own pleasure, that my bedroom derived its beauty. The tall white curtains which hid from view the bed, set back as if in a sanctuary; the scattering of marceline quilts, flowered counterpanes, embroidered bedspreads, and batiste pillow-slips beneath which it disappeared during the day, like an altar beneath its flowers and festoons in the month of Mary, and which, in the evening, so that I could get into bed, I would lay cautiously down on an armchair where they consented to spend the night; beside the bed, the trinity of the glass with its blue designs, the matching sugar bowl and the water-jug (empty ever since the day following my arrival on the orders of my aunt, who was afraid to have me 'upsetting' it), like the implements of some religion – almost as holy as the precious orange-blossom liqueur sitting next to them in a glass phial – which I would no more have thought myself permitted to profane or even possible to make use of for my own personal ends than if they had been consecrated ciboria, but which I contemplated at length before getting undressed, for fear of upsetting them by some false movement; the little crochet-work stoles which cast a mantle of white roses over the backs of the armchairs and which cannot have been thornless because, whenever I had finished reading and tried to stand up, I noticed I was still hooked on to them; the glass dome beneath which, immured from vulgar contact, the clock chattered intimately away for the seashells brought from afar and for an old sentimental flower, but which was so heavy to lift up that when the clock stopped, no one, except the clockmaker, would have been rash enough to undertake to rewind it; the white point-lace cloth which had been thrown like an altar-covering over the commode decorated with two vases, a picture of the Saviour and a palm-frond, making it look like the Communion Table (the evocation of which was completed by a prie-dieu, put away there every day when the bedroom was 'done'), but whose frayed ends were perpetually catching in the cracks of the drawers and stopping them so completely from working that I could never take out a handkerchief without all at once bringing down the picture of the Saviour, the holy vases, and the palm-frond, and without myself stumbling and holding on to the prie-dieu; the triple thickness finally of thin butter-cloth curtains, heavy muslin curtains and still heavier damask curtains, always cheerful and white as the mayblossom and often with the sun on them, yet fundamentally most annoying in the clumsy, obstinate way they moved around their parallel wooden rods and became caught one in the other and all of them together in the window the moment I wanted to open or close it, a second one being ever ready, if I had succeeded in freeing a first, immediately to take its place in the joins, which they stopped up as completely as a real hawthorn bush might have done or the nests of swallows that had taken it into their heads to build there, with the result that I could never manage this apparently very simple operation, of opening or closing my casement, without help from a member of the household; all these objects which not only could not answer to any of my needs but which actually placed an obstacle, albeit slight, in the way of their satisfaction, and which had obviously never been put there to be useful to anyone, peopled my bedroom with thoughts that were somehow personal, with that air of predilection of having chosen to live and enjoy themselves there which trees often have in a clearing, or flowers by the roadside or on old walls. They filled it with a diverse and silent life, with a mystery in which my person was at once lost and entranced; they made that bedroom into a sort of chapel where the sunshine – once it had passed through the little panes of red glass which my uncle had inserted into the tops of the windows, – after turning the mayblossom of the curtains to pink, speckled the walls with glimmerings as strange as if the little chapel had been enclosed within a larger nave of stained-glass; and where the sound of the bells reached one so resonantly, our house being close to the church, to which we were joined moreover, on high feast-days, by the floral way of the altars of rest, that I could fancy that they were being rung in our own roof, just above the window from which I would often greet the priest with his breviary, or my aunt on her way back from vespers, or the choirboy bringing us consecrated bread. As for the photograph by Brown of Botticelli's 'Spring' or the cast of the 'Unknown Woman' from the museum in Lille, which were William Morris's concession to a useless beauty on the walls and mantel-pieces of Maple's bedrooms, I have to confess that in my bedroom they had been replaced by a sort of engraving showing Prince Eugène, handsome and terrible in his dolman, which I was greatly astonished to catch sight of one night, amidst a great crashing of locomotives and hailstones, still handsome and terrible, in the entrance to a station buffet, where it was serving as an advertisement for a make of biscuits. Nowadays I suspect my grandfather of having got it in the old days as a bonus from a generous manufacturer, before installing it permanently in my bedroom. But at that time I was unconcerned by its origins, which seemed to me historical and mysterious, and I did not imagine that there might be several copies of what I looked on as a person, as a permanent inhabitant of the room which I merely shared with him and where every year I rediscovered him, forever the same. It is a long time now since I saw him, and I suppose that I shall never see him again. But were such good fortune to befall me, I believe he would have many more things to say to me than Botticelli's 'Spring'. I leave it to people of taste to decorate their homes with reproductions of the masterpieces which they admire and to relieve their memories of the trouble of preserving a precious image for them by entrusting it to a carved wooden frame. I leave it to people of taste to make of their bedrooms the very image of their taste and to fill them only with those objects of which it can approve. For myself, I only feel myself live and think in a room where everything is the creation and the language of lives profoundly different from my own, of a taste the opposite of mine, where I can rediscover nothing of my conscious thought, where my imagination is exhilarated by feeling itself plunged into the heart of the non-self; I only feel happy when I set foot – in the Avenue de la Gare, overlooking the harbour, or in the Place de l'Eglise

– in one of those provincial hotels with long cold corridors where the wind from outside is winning the battle against the efforts of the central heating, where the detailed map of the locality is still the only decoration on the walls, where each sound serves only to make the silence apparent by displacing it, where the bedrooms preserve a musty aroma which the fresh air washes away but cannot erase, and that the nostrils breathe in a hundred times to carry it to the imagination, which is enchanted by it and makes it pose as a model to try and recreate it within itself with all it contains by way of thoughts and memories; where in the evenings, when you open the door of your bedroom, you feel you are violating all the life that remains dispersed there, taking it boldly by the hand as, the door once closed, you enter further in, up to the table or the window; that you are sitting in a sort of free promiscuity with it on a settee made by the upholsterer in the county town in what he believed was the Parisian style; that you are everywhere touching the bareness of this life in the intention of disturbing yourself by your own familiarity, as you put your things down in this place or that, playing the proprietor in a room filled to overflowing with the souls of others and which preserves the imprint of their dreams in the very shape of the firedogs or the pattern on the curtains, or as you walk barefoot over its unknown carpet; then you have the sense of locking this secret life in with you, as you go, trembling all over, to bolt the door; of driving it ahead of you into the bed and at last of lying down with it in the great white sheets which come up above your face, while, close by, the church tolls for the whole town the hours that are without sleep for lovers and for the dying.

I had not been reading in my room for very long before having to go to the park, a kilometre out of the village. But this enforced playtime over, I would cut short the end of tea, which had been brought in baskets and handed out to the children by the river bank, on the grass where my book had been laid with orders not to pick it up again. A little further on, in certain rather overgrown and rather mysterious reaches of the park, the river ceased from being an artificial, rectilinear water-course, covered with swans and lined by paths of cheerful statues, and skipping now and again with carp, and gathered speed, flowed rapidly on past the enclosure of the park to become a river in the geographical sense of the word – a river which must have had a name – and to lose no time in spreading itself out (was it really the same one as between the statues and beneath the swans?) between pastures where cattle slept and whose butter-cups it had drowned, a sort of meadowland it had made quite marshy, attached on one side to the village by some shapeless towers, remains it was said, of the Middle Ages, while on the other side it was joined, up climbing paths of eglantine and hawthorn, to 'nature', which stretched away into infinity, villages which had other names, the unknown. I would leave the others to finish having tea at the bottom of the park, beside the swans, and run up into the maze as far as some arbour or other and there sit, unfindable, my back against the clipped hazel bushes, taking note of the asparagus bed, the edging of strawberry plants, the ornamental lake up into which, on certain days, the water would be pumped by circling horses, the white gate at the top which was the 'end of the park' and, beyond it, the fields of poppies and cornflowers. In my arbour the silence was profound, the risk of being discovered negligible, my security made all the sweeter by the distant shouts summoning me in vain from down below, which at times even drew closer, mounted the first banks, searching everywhere, but then turned back again, not having found; then, no further sound; only, from time to time, the golden notes of the bells that, far away, beyond the plains, seemed to be ringing out behind the blue sky and might have warned me that time was passing; but surprised by their softness and troubled by the deeper silence, emptied of their last notes that ensued, I was never certain of the number of strokes. These were not the thunderous bells you heard when re-entering the village – as you approached the church which, from close to, had resumed its tall, rigid stature, its slate cowl punctuated by corbels standing up against the blue of the evening – shivering the sound into splinters on the village square 'for the good things of the earth'. They were soft and feeble by the time they reached the end of the park and being directed not at me, but at the whole countryside, at all the villages, at the country people isolated in their fields, they in no way obliged me to look up but passed close beside me, carrying the time to distant places, without seeing me, or recognizing me, or disturbing me.

And sometimes in the house, in my bed, long after dinner, the last hours of the evening would also give shelter to my reading, but only on days when I had come to the last chapters of a book, when there was not much to be read before getting to the end. Then, at the risk of being punished if I was discovered, or of an insomnia which might last right through the night once the book was finished, as soon as my parents were in bed I relit my candle; while in the street nearby, between the gunsmith's house and the post office, both steeped in silence, the dark yet blue sky was full of stars, and to the left, above the raised alley-way where one began the winding ascent to it, you could sense the monstrous black apse of the church to be watching, whose sculptures did not sleep at night, a village church yet a historic one, the magical dwelling-place of the Good Lord, of the con-secrated loaf, of the multicoloured saints and of the ladies from the neighbouring châteaux who set the hens squawking and the gossips staring as they crossed the marketplace on feast-days, when they came to mass 'in their turn-outs', and who, on their way home, just after they had emerged from the shadow of the porch where the faithful were scattering the vagrant rubies of the nave as they pushed open the door of the vestibule, did not fail to buy from the pâtissier in the square some of those cakes shaped like towers, which were protected from the sunlight by a blind – 'manqués', 'saint-honorés' and 'genoa cakes', whose indolent, sugary aroma has remained mingled for me with the bells for high mass and the gaiety of Sundays.

Then the last page had been read, the book was finished. The frantic career of the eyes and of the voice which had been following them, noiselessly, pausing only to catch its breath, had to be halted, in a deep sigh.

And then, so as to give the turbulence loose inside me for too long to be able to still itself other movements to control, I would get up and start walking up and down by my bed, my eyes still fixed on some point that might have been looked for in vain either inside the room or without, for it was the distance of a soul away, one of those distances not to be measured in metres or in miles, unlike others, and which it is impossible moreover to mistake for them once one sees the 'remote' stare of those whose thoughts are 'elsewhere'. Was there no more to the book than this, then? These creatures on whom one had bestowed more attention and affection than on those in real life, not always daring to admit to what extent you loved them, and even, when my parents found me reading and seemed to smile at my emotion, closing the book with studied indifference or a pretence of boredom; never again would one see these people for whom one had sobbed and yearned, never again hear of them. Already, in the last few pages, the author himself, in his cruel 'Epilogue', had been careful to 'space them out' with an indifference not to be credited by anyone who knew the interest with which he had followed them hitherto, step by step. The occupation of each hour of their lives had been narrated to us. Then, all of a sudden: 'Twenty years after these events an old man might have been met with in the rue des Fougères, still erect, etc.'[1] And the marriage, the delightful possibility of which we have been enabled to glimpse through two whole volumes, fearful at first and then overjoyed as each obstacle was raised and then smoothed away, we learn from a casual phrase by some minor character that it has been celebrated, we do not know exactly when, in this astonishing epilogue written, it would seem, from up in heaven, by someone indifferent to our momentary passions who has taken the author's place. One would have so much liked for the book to continue or, if that was impossible, to have other facts about all these characters, to learn something of their lives now, to employ our own on things not altogether unconnected with the love they have inspired in us,[2] whose object was now all of a sudden gone from us, not to have loved in vain, for an hour, human beings who tomorrow will be no more than a name on a forgotten page, in a book unrelated to our lives and as to whose value we were certainly mistaken since its fate here below, as we could now see and as our parents had taught us when need arose by a dismissive phrase, was not at all, as we had thought, to contain the universe and our own destiny, but to occupy a very narrow space in the lawyer's book-case, between the unglamorous archives of the *Journal de modes illustré* and *La Géographie d'Eure-et-Loir*.

Before attempting to show, on the threshold to 'Of Kings' Treasuries', why in my opinion Reading should not play the preponderant role in life assigned to it by Ruskin in this little work, I needed to make an exception for that delightful childhood reading the memory of which must remain a benediction for each one of us. No doubt the length and nature of the preceding exposition proves only too well what I had first of all claimed for it: that what it chiefly leaves behind in us is the image of the places and the times when we did it. I have not escaped from its spell; I wanted to speak of my reading but I have spoken of everything except books because it was not of them that my reading spoke to me. But perhaps the memories it has given me back, one after the other, will themselves have awakened in my reader and led him gradually, as he dwelt along these flowery, circuitous paths, to recreate in his own mind the original psychological act known as *Reading*, sufficiently strongly for him to be able now to follow, as if within himself, the few reflections it remains to me to proffer.

We know that 'Of Kings' Treasuries' was a lecture on reading given by Ruskin in the town hall of Rusholme, near Manchester, on 6 December 1864, to help in the setting-up of a library at the Rusholme Institute. On 14 December he gave a second, 'Of Queens' Gardens', about the role of women, to help found schools in Ancoats. 'All through that year,' says Mr Collingwood in his admirable *Life and Work of Ruskin*, 'he remained at home, except for . . . frequent evenings with Carlyle. And when, in December, he gave those lectures in Manchester which afterwards, as *Sesame and Lilies*, became his most popular work, we can trace his better health of mind and body in the brighter tone of his thought. We can hear the echo of Carlyle's talk in the heroic, aristocratic, stoic ideals, and in the insistence on the value of books and free public libraries, – Carlyle being the founder of the London Library.'

Since all I wish to do here is to discuss Ruskin's thesis in itself, without concerning myself with its historical origins, it may be summed up quite accurately in the words of Descartes, that 'the reading of all good books is like a conversation with the worthiest individuals of past centuries who were their authors.' Ruskin did not perhaps know of this somewhat arid reflection of the French philosopher, but it is one in point of fact which is to be found throughout his lecture, only swathed in an Apollonian gold fused with the mists of England, like those whose splendour illuminates the landscapes of his favourite painter. 'But, granting that we had both the will and the sense to choose our friends well, how few of us have the power! or, at least, how limited, for most, is the sphere of choice! . . . We cannot know whom we would . . . We may, by good fortune, obtain a glimpse of a great poet, and hear the sound of his voice; or put a question to a man of science, and be answered good-humouredly. We may intrude ten minutes' talk on a cabinet minister, . . . or snatch, once or twice in our lives, the privilege of . . . arresting the kind glance of a Queen. And yet these momentary chances we covet; and spend our years, passions, and powers in pursuit of little more than these; while, meantime, there is a society continually open to us, of people who will talk to us as long as we like, whatever our rank or occupation; . . . And this society, because it is so numerous and so gentle, – and can be kept waiting round us all day long, not to grant audience but to gain it – kings and statesmen lingering patiently in those plainly furnished and narrow anterooms, our bookcase shelves, – we make no account of that company, – perhaps never listen to a word they would say, all day long!' 'You may tell me perhaps,' adds Ruskin, 'that if you prefer to talk with the living, it is because you can see their faces,' etc., and rebutting this

first objection, and then a second, he shows that reading
is precisely a conversation with men much wiser and
more interesting than those whom we may have
occasion to meet with around us. In the notes which I
have added to this volume I have tried to show that
reading cannot be assimilated in this way to a conversation, even with the wisest of men; that the difference
essentially between a book and a friend lies not in their
greater or lesser wisdom, but in the manner in which
we communicate with them, reading being the reverse
of conversation, consisting as it does for each one of us
in receiving the communication of another's thought
while still being on our own, that is, continuing to enjoy
the intellectual sway which we have in solitude and
which conversation dispels instantly, and continuing to
be open to inspiration, with our minds still at work hard
and fruitfully on themselves. Had Ruskin drawn the
consequences of other truths which he states a few pages
later on, he would probably have reached a conclusion
analogous to my own. But obviously he was not seeking
to get to the very heart of the idea of *reading*. In order
to teach us the value of reading, he seeks only to recount
a sort of beautiful Platonic myth, with the simplicity of
the Greeks who showed us almost all the true ideas and
left it to modern scruples to explore them more fully.
But although I think that reading, in its original essence,
in the fertile miracle of a communication effected in
solitude, is something more, and something other than
what Ruskin says that it is, I do not for all that think that
one can allow it the preponderant role in our spiritual
lives which he seems to assign to it.

The limitations of its role derive from the nature of its virtues. And it is to my childhood reading once again that I shall go to find out in what these virtues consist. The book which you saw me reading just now beside the fire in the dining-room, in my bedroom, in the depths of the armchair with its crocheted head-rest, or on fine afternoons, beneath the nut trees and hawthorns in the park, where every breath from the boundless fields came from so far off to play silently at my side, holding mutely out to my distracted nostrils the scent of the clover and the sainfoin to which my weary eyes would sometimes be raised: that book, since your eyes as you lean towards it would be unable to make out its title across those twenty years, my memory, whose eyesight is better suited to this kind of perception, will tell you what it was: *Le Capitaine Fracasse*, by Théophile Gautier. In it I loved before all else two or three sentences which seemed to me the most beautiful and original in the book. I could not imagine that any other author had written comparable ones. But I had the feeling that their beauty corresponded to a reality of which Théophile Gautier allowed us to glimpse only a small corner once or twice in each volume. And as I believed that he must assuredly know it in its entirety, I would have liked to read other books by him in which all the sentences would be as beautiful as these and would have as their subject the things on which I would have liked to have his opinion. 'Laughter is not cruel by its nature; it distinguishes man from the animals and is, so it appears from the *Odyssey* of Homerus, the Grecian poet, the prerogative of the blessed and immortal gods who laugh their Olympian fill as they lounge away eternity.'[3] This sentence produced a genuine intoxication in me. I thought I caught sight of a marvellous antiquity through the Middle Ages as Gautier alone could reveal them to me. But I would have wished that instead of saying this furtively, after the tedious description of a château containing too many terms I did not know for me to be at all able to visualize it, he had written sentences of this kind all through the volume and spoken to me of things that once his book was finished I could continue to know and to love. I would have wished for him, the one wise custodian of the truth, to tell me what I ought rightly to think of Shakespeare, of Saintine, of Sophocles, of Euripides, of Silvio Pellico whom I had read one very cold March, walking, stamping my feet, running along the paths, whenever I had just closed the book, exhilarated by having finished my reading, by the energy accumulated by my immobility, and by the salubrious wind blowing down the village streets. I would have wished him above all to tell me whether I would have a better chance of arriving at the truth if I repeated my first-form year at school or later on by becoming a diplomat or an advocate at the Court of Appeal. But as soon as the beautiful sentence was finished he set to describing a table covered 'with a layer of dust so thick that a finger might have traced letters in it', too insignificant a thing in my eyes for me to be able even to let my attention pause at it; and I was reduced to wondering what other books Gautier had written which might better satisfy my aspirations and enable me finally to know the whole of his thought.

Indeed, it is one of the great and wonderful characteristics of good books (which will give us to see the role at once essential yet limited that reading may play in our spiritual lives) that for the author they may be called 'Conclusions' but for the reader 'Incitements'. We feel very strongly that our own wisdom begins where that of the author leaves off, and we would like him to provide us with answers when all he is able to do is to provide us with desires. And he can only awaken these desires by making us contemplate the supreme beauty to which the utmost efforts of his art have enabled him to attain. But by a singular and moreover providential law of mental optics (a law which signifies perhaps that we are unable to receive the truth from anyone else but must create it ourselves), the end-point of their wisdom appears to us only as the beginning of our own, so that it is at the moment when they have told us everything they could have told us that they give rise to the feeling in us that as yet they have told us nothing. Moreover, if we put questions to them which they are unable to answer, we also ask them for answers which would teach us nothing. For an effect of the love which poets arouse in us is to make us attach a literal importance to things significant to them only of personal emotions. In each picture that they show us, they seem to afford us only a brief glimpse of some marvellous location, different from the rest of the world, and we would like them to make us enter into the very heart of it. 'Take us,' we would like to be able to say to M. Maeterlinck or Mme de Noailles, ' "into the Zeeland garden where the old-fashioned flowers grow", along the highway scented "with clover and artemisia", and into all those places on the earth of which you have not spoken in your books but which you adjudge to be as beautiful as these.' We would like to go and visit the field which Millet (for painters teach us in the same manner as poets) shows us in his 'Springtime', we would like M. Claude Monet to take us to Giverny, on the Seine, to that bend in the river which he allows us barely to make out through the morning mist. Yet, in actual fact, it was the mere chance of an acquaintance or family connection which gave Mme de Noailles, or Maeterlinck, or Millet, or Claude Monet occasion to pass or to stay nearby and made them choose to paint that road, that garden, that field, that bend in the river rather than another. What makes them seem other and more beautiful to us than the rest of the world is that they bear on them like some elusive reflection the impression they made on a genius, and which we might see wandering just as singular and despotic across the submissive and indifferent face of all the landscapes he may have painted. This surface with which they charm and disappoint us, and beyond which we would like to go, is the very essence of that in a sense depthless thing – a mirage arrested on a canvas – which is a vision. And the mist which our eager eyes would like to pierce is the last word in the painter's art. The supreme effort of the writer as of the artist only succeeds in raising partially for us the veil of ugliness and insignificance that leaves us incurious before the universe. Then does he say: 'Look, look,

Parfumés de trèfle et d'armoise
Serrant leurs vifs ruisseaux étroits
Les pays de l'Aisne et de l'Oise.

Scented with clover and artemisia
Gripping their quick, narrow streams
The country of the Aisne and of the Oise.

'Look at the house in Zeeland, pink and shiny as a seashell. Look! Learn to see!' At which moment he disappears. That is the value of reading, and also its inadequacy. To make it into a discipline is to give too large a role to what is only an incitement. Reading is on the threshold of the spiritual life; it can introduce us to it: it does not constitute it.

There are certain cases, however, certain as it were pathological cases of spiritual depression, when reading may become a sort of healing discipline and be entrusted, by way of repeated incitements, with reintroducing a lazy mind perpetually into the life of the spirit. Then books play a role for it analogous to that of psychotherapists for certain cases of neurasthenia.

We know that in certain affections of the nervous system, without any of the organs themselves being affected, the patient is mired in a sort of impossibility of willing, as if in a deep rut, from which he cannot escape unaided and where ultimately he would waste away, if a strong and helping hand were not held out to him. His brain, his legs, his lungs, his stomach are sound. He is not truly incapacitated from working, from walking, from exposing himself to the cold, from eating. But he is incapable of willing these various actions, which he would be perfectly capable of performing. And an organic degeneration, which would end by becoming the equivalent of the diseases he does not have, would be the irremediable consequence of this inertia of the will, if the impulsion he is unable to find in himself were not to come to him from outside, from a doctor who will will for him, until such time as his various organic wills have been re-educated. Now there exist certain minds that might be compared to patients such as these, who are prevented by a sort of laziness[4] or frivolity from descending spontaneously into the deeper parts of the self where the true life of the spirit begins. It is not that once they have been shown the way there they are incapable of discovering and exploiting its true riches, but that, failing such intervention from without, they live on the surface in a perpetual forgetfulness of themselves, in a sort of passivity which makes them the plaything of every pleasure and reduces them to the stature of those roundabout who excite them, so that, like the man of gentle birth who, having shared the life of highway robbers ever since childhood, could not remember his name any more so long ago was it that he had ceased to bear it, they would end by abolishing in themselves all sense and recollection of their spiritual nobility, were an outside impulsion not to come to reintroduce them forcibly in a sense into the life of the mind, where they suddenly recover the power of thinking for themselves and of creating. Now it is clear that this impulsion, which the lazy mind cannot find in itself but which has to come to it from another, must be received in that solitude outside of which, as we have seen, the very activity of creation that is to be resuscitated cannot occur. From pure solitude the lazy mind can derive nothing, since it is incapable of setting its creative activity in motion of its own accord. But the most lofty conversation and the most pressing advice are of no assistance to it either, for they cannot produce this original activity directly. What it takes then, is an intervention which, though it comes from someone else, occurs deep inside ourselves, the impulsion certainly of another mind but received in the midst of our solitude. But we have already seen that this was exactly the definition of reading, and applicable to reading alone. Thus the one discipline that can exercise a favourable influence on such minds is reading: *quod erat demonstrandum*, as the geometers say. But here again, reading works only as an incitement which can in no way take the place of our own personal activity; it is content simply to restore the use of it to us, just as, in the nervous ailments to which I was alluding a little earlier, the psychotherapist merely restores to the patient the willpower to make use of his still sound stomach, legs and brain. Whether it is that all minds have more or less of such laziness, of this stagnation of the lower depths, or whether, though it may not be essential, the exaltation that some reading can produce has a propitious influence on our own work, more than one writer is quoted as having liked to read some choice extract before sitting down to work. Emerson seldom began to write without having reread a few pages of Plato. And Dante is not the only poet whom Virgil has conducted to the threshold of paradise.

For as long as reading is for us the instigator whose magic keys have opened the door to those dwelling-places deep within us that we would not have known how to enter, its role in our lives is salutary. It becomes dangerous on the other hand, when, instead of awakening us to the personal life of the mind, reading tends to take its place, when the truth no longer appears to us as an ideal which we can realize only by the intimate progress of our own thought and the efforts of our own heart, but as something material, deposited between the leaves of books like a honey fully prepared by others and which we need only take the trouble to reach down from the shelves of libraries and then sample passively in a perfect repose of mind and body. Sometimes even, in certain somewhat exceptional and anyway, as we shall see, less dangerous cases, the truth, still conceived of as something external, is at a distance from us, concealed in a place difficult of access. Then it is some secret document, some unpublished correspondence, some memoir which may shed an unexpected light on certain characters, but which can be imparted to us only with difficulty. What happiness, what respite for the mind weary of seeking within for the truth to tell itself that it is to be found without, in the sheets of an in-folio jealously preserved in a convent in Holland, and that though it may cost us some effort to come at it, this will be a purely material effort and no more than a charming relaxation for the mind. It will mean a long journey by passenger barge, no doubt, across fenlands moaning with the wind, as on the bank the reeds bend and straighten by turns in an endless undulation; it will mean stopping in Dordrecht, whose ivy-clad church will be mirrored in the tangle of dormant canals and in the golden, tremulous Meuse, where in the evening the boats, as they glide past, break up the reflections of the lines of red roofs and the blue sky; and when at last we come to our destination, we shall still not be certain of being given the truth. For that, powerful influences must be brought into play and friends made with the venerable Archbishop of Utrecht, his handsome square face like that of an old Jansenist, and with the pious keeper of the archives in Amersfoort. In such instances the conquest of the truth is seen as the triumph of a sort of diplomatic mission in which the journey was not without its difficulties nor the negotiation without its hazards. But what matter? All these members of the little old church in Utrecht, on whose good will our entering into possession of the truth depends, are charming folk whose seventeenth-century faces make a change from those we are used to and with whom it will be most amusing to remain in touch, at least by letter. The esteem with which, from time to time, they will continue to send us their evidence will raise us in our own eyes and we shall keep their letters as a warranty and as a curiosity. And we shall not fail one day to dedicate one of our books to them, which is certainly the least one can do for people who have made one a gift . . . of the truth. And as for the few enquiries, the brief labour that we shall be obliged to undertake in the library of the convent, and which will be the indispensable prelude to the act of entering on possession of the truth – that truth on which, for prudence's sake and so as not to risk its escaping from us, we shall take notes – it would be ungrateful to complain of the pains they may have cost us: the peace and coolness of the old convent are so exquisite, where the nuns still wear the tall headdresses with white wings that they have in the Roger van der Weyden in the visiting-room; and as we are working the seventeenth-century carillons fondly take the chill off the artless waters of the canal, which a little pale sunlight is sufficient to make to dazzle us between the double row of trees, bare since the summer ended, that brush against the mirrors hanging from the gabled houses on either bank.[5]

This conception of a truth deaf to the appeals of reflection but docile to the exercise of influence, of a truth to be obtained through letters of recommendation, which is put into our hands by whoever had charge of it materially without perhaps even knowing of it, of a truth which allows itself to be copied out into a notebook, such a conception of the truth is yet far from being the most dangerous of all. Because very often, for the historian and even for the scholar, the truth which they go to seek far away in a book is not so much the truth itself, properly speaking, as its index or its proof, leaving room consequently for another truth of which it is the promise or the verification and which is, this time at least, an individual creation of their own minds. It is not at all the same for the literary man. He reads in order to read, to retain what he has read. For him the book is not the angel who takes wing the moment he has opened the gates into the celestial garden, but a motionless idol, which he adores for its own sake and which, instead of acquiring a true dignity from the thoughts it arouses, communicates a factitious dignity to everything around it. The literary man invokes it smilingly in honour of some name to be found in Villehardouin or in Boccaccio,[6] or in favour of some custom described in Virgil. His mind has no original activity of its own and is unable to pick out in books the substance which might fortify it; it encumbers itself with them as a whole so that, instead of being an assimilable element for him, a principle of life, they are merely a foreign body, a principle of death. Is there any need to say that if I qualify this fondness, this sort of fetishistic reverence for books as unhealthy, it is relative to what the ideal habits of a mind without defects would be, which does not exist, just as physiologists do who describe the normal workings of organs such as are hardly to be met with in living persons. In real life, on the contrary, where there are no perfect minds any more than entirely healthy bodies, those whom we call great minds are afflicted as others are by this 'literary disease'. More so than others, one might say. It seems that the liking for books grows along with the intellect, a little below it but on the same stem, just as any passion goes with a predilection for what surrounds its object, has some connection with it and still speaks of it in its absence. And so the greatest writers, at those times when they are not in direct communication with their own thought, take pleasure in the company of books. Is it not above all for them, moreover, that they were written; do they not disclose to them untold beauties which remain hidden from the masses? But in truth, the fact that superior minds may be what one terms bookish in no way proves that this is not a failing in someone. From the fact that mediocre men are often industrious and intelligent ones often lazy, one cannot conclude that hard work is not a better discipline for the mind than laziness. In spite of which, to meet with one of our own faults in a great man always sets us to wondering whether it was not at bottom an unacknowledged virtue, and it is not without pleasure that we learn that Hugo knew Quintus Curtius, Tacitus and Justinian by heart, and that if the legitimacy of a word was challenged in his presence he was quite ready to trace its genealogy back to its origins, by quotations that demonstrated a genuine erudition. (I have shown elsewhere how in his case this erudition fostered his genius instead of stifling it, just as a bundle of sticks may put out a small fire but helps a large one.) Maeterlinck, who is for me the opposite of a literary man, whose mind is perpetually open to the countless anonymous emotions conveyed by the beehive, the flowerbed or the pasture, reassures us largely as to the dangers of erudition, and almost of bibliophilia, when he describes as an amateur the engravings decorating an old edition of Jacob Cats or the Abbé Sanderus. These dangers, when they exist, are anyway much less of a threat to our intellect than to our sensibility, and the capacity to read with profit is, if I may so express it, much greater among thinkers than among imaginative writers. Schopenhauer for example, offers us the image of a mind whose vitality wears the most enormous reading lightly, each new item of knowledge being at once reduced to its element of reality, to the portion of life that it contains.

Schopenhauer never puts forward an opinion without

at once supporting it by several quotations, but one has the feeling that for him the texts he cites are merely examples, unconscious or anticipatory allusions in which he likes to discover a few features of his own thought but which have in no way been his inspiration. I recall a passage in *The World as Will and Idea* where there are perhaps twenty quotations in a row. The subject is pessimism (I will abridge the quotations, naturally): 'Voltaire, in *Candide*, wages war on optimism in an agreeable manner. Byron did so, in his tragic style, in *Cain*. Herodotus reports that the Thracians greeted the newborn with lamentations and rejoiced at each death. This is what is expressed in the lovely lines that Plutarch records: *Lugere genitum, tanta, qui intravit mala*, etc. To which must be attributed the custom among the Mexicans of wishing, etc., and Swift was obeying the same sentiment when from his young days on (if Sir Walter Scott's biography is to be believed) he was accustomed to celebrating the day of his birth as a day of affliction. Everyone knows the passage in Plato's *Apology* where he says that death is a good to be admired. A maxim of Heraclitus is similarly framed: *Vitae nomen quidam est vita, opus autem mors*. As for the lovely lines of Theognis, they are famous: *Optima sors homini natum non esse*, etc. Sophocles in *Oedipus at Colonus*, summarizes it as follows: *Natum non esse sortes vincit alias omnes*, etc. Euripides says: *Omnis hominum vita est plena dolore* (*Hippolytus*), and Homer had already said it: *Non enim quidquam alicubi est calamitosius homine omnium, quotquot super terram spirant*, etc. Pliny said so too, moreover: *Nullum melius esse tempestiva morte*. Shakespeare puts these words into the mouth of the old king Henry IV:

'Oh if this were seen – The happiest youth – Would shut the book and sit him down and die.' Byron finally: " 'Tis something better not to be." Balthasar Gracián paints existence for us in the blackest colours, including the *Criticón*, etc.' Had I not already let myself be carried too far by Schopenhauer, I would have been happy to round off this little demonstration with the help of *Aphorisms on Wisdom in Life*, which is of all the books known to me perhaps the one which presupposes in its author the most originality along with the widest reading, so that at the head of the book, each page of which contains several quotations, Schopenhauer was able to write in all seriousness: 'Compilation is not my forte.'

Friendship, friendship in respect of individuals, is no doubt a frivolous thing, and reading is a form of friendship. But at least it is a sincere form, and the fact that it is directed at someone who is dead, who is not there, lends something disinterested, almost moving to it. It is a form of friendship freed moreover from all that makes other forms ugly. Since we are all of us, the living, but dead people who have not yet taken up their appointment, all those politenesses, all those salutations in the entrance-hall that we call deference, or gratitude, or devotion, and into which we mix so much falsehood, are wearisome and sterile. What is more – from our very first relations of sympathy, admiration or gratitude – the first words that we utter, the first letters we write weave around us the first threads of a canvas of habit, of a veritable mode of existence, which we are no longer able to rid ourselves of in our subsequent friendships; not to mention that during this time the excessive things we have said remain like promissory notes that we must settle, or that we shall pay for even more dearly all through our lives by our remorse at having allowed them to be protested. In reading, friendship is suddenly brought back to its original purity. There is no false amiability with books. If we spend the evening with these friends, it is because we genuinely want to. We often take leave of them, at least, only with regret. And once we have left them, none of those thoughts that spoil friendship: 'What did they think of us?' 'Were we not tactless?' 'Did they like us?' or the fear of being forgotten in favour of someone else. All these qualms of friendship expire on the threshold of the pure and peaceful form of it that is reading. There is no deference either, we laugh at what Molière has to say only just so far as we find it funny; when he bores us we are not afraid to look bored, and once we have definitely had enough of him we put him back in his place as abruptly as if he had neither genius nor celebrity. The atmosphere of this pure form of friendship is silence, which is purer than speech. Because we speak for others, but remain silent for ourselves. So silence, unlike speech, does not bear the trace of our faults or affectations. It is pure, it is genuinely an atmosphere. Between the author's thought and our own it does not interpose the irreducible elements, refractory to thought, of our two distinct egos. The very language of the book is pure (if it is worthy to be called a book), made transparent by the thought of the author, which has removed whatever was not itself to make of it its own faithful image; each sentence, at bottom, resembling the others, because all are spoken with the unique inflection of a personality; hence a sort of continuity that in life our commerce with others excludes by mixing in with our own thought elements foreign to it, and which very quickly enables us to follow the actual line of the author's thought, the features of his physiognomy as they are reflected in this tranquil mirror. We are able to take pleasure in the features of each one in turn, without asking that they be admirable, for the mind delights in making out these profound portraits and loving them with an unselfish, unassuming friendship, as if for their own sake. Thus do we take to a Gautier, simple, a good fellow, with excellent taste (it amuses me to think that they could see him as representing perfection in art). I do not overestimate his spiritual capacities, and in his *Voyage en Espagne*, where every sentence, without his suspecting it, stresses and extends the very graceful, very cheerful line of his personality (the words arranging themselves of their own accord to trace it, because his personality it was that chose them and set them out in order), I cannot help but see as anything but true art the obligation he felt himself to be under not to let a single form go by without a full description, and accompanied by a comparison which does not originate in any strong or agreeable impression and is therefore by no means appealing. When he likens the countryside with its different forms of cultivation 'to those tailors' cards which have samples of trousers and waistcoats stuck down on them', one can but blame the pitiful poverty of his imagination, as when he says that there is nothing to admire between Paris and Angoulême. And one smiles at this fervent Gothicist who could not even be bothered in Chartres to go and visit the cathedral. ('I regret having passed through Chartres without managing to see the cathedral', *Voyage en Espagne*.)

But what good humour and what taste! how willingly we follow this very buoyant companion on his adventures; so sympathetic is he that we find everything around him so too. And after the few days he spends with Captain Lebarbier de Tinan, delayed by the storm on board his fine vessel, 'glistening like gold', we are sad he should have nothing more to say about that amiable sailor but makes us take leave of him for ever without telling us what became of him.[7] One certainly has the sense that his cheerful bragging like his fits of melancholy were in his case the somewhat unbuttoned habits of the journalist. But we give him all that, we do what he wants, we are amused when he comes home soaked to the skin, dying of hunger and for some sleep, and sad when, as mournfully as any *feuilletoniste*, he recites the names of all those men of his own generation dead before their time. I was saying about him that his sentences traced his physiognomy but without his suspecting it; for if words are chosen, not by our minds in accordance with the affinities of their essence, but by our desire to portray ourselves, he represents that desire, he does not represent us. For all their gifts, Fromentin and Musset, because they wanted to leave their own portraits to posterity, painted them very indifferently; yet they interest us enormously for that very reason, because their failure is instructive. So that even when a book is not the mirror of a powerful individuality, it is still the mirror of interesting defects in the mind. When we read closely a book by Fromentin or a book by Musset, we notice in the first how fundamentally limited and stupid a certain 'distinction' is, and in the second how vacuous is eloquence.

If, as we grow intellectually, our liking for books grows also, its dangers, as we have seen, are reduced. An original mind is able to subordinate its reading to its own personal activity. For it, reading is merely the noblest of distractions, above all the most ennobling, for reading and knowledge alone make for a 'well-mannered' mind. We can only develop the power of our sensibility and our intellect in ourselves, in the depths of our spiritual lives. But it is in this contact with other minds that is reading that the 'ways' of our minds are inculcated. In spite of everything, the well-read remain the intellectual 'quality' as it were, and not to know a particular book, or a particular item of literary knowledge, will always be, even in a man of genius, a mark of intellectual ill-breeding. In the order of the mind too, distinction and nobility consist in a sort of freemasonry of usage and a heritage of traditions.[8]

The preference of great writers, in this taste and diversion of reading, is very readily given to books by the ancients. Even those whom their contemporaries saw as the most 'romantic' read hardly anything except the classics. When, in conversation, Victor Hugo talks about what he has been reading, it is the names of Molière, of Horace, of Ovid, of Régnard, which recur the most frequently. Alphonse Daudet, the least bookish of writers, whose oeuvre is so thoroughly vital and modern it seems to have rejected the whole classical inheritance, was ceaselessly reading, quoting, glossing Pascal, Montaigne, Diderot, Tacitus.[9] One might almost go so far as to say, so renewing perhaps, by an anyway wholly partial interpretation, the old distinction between classics and romantics, that it is audiences (intelligent audiences, of course) which are romantic, whereas the masters (even the masters said to be romantic, those preferred by romantic audiences) are classic. (An observation that could be extended to all the arts. The public goes to hear the music of M. Vincent d'Indy, M. Vincent d'Indy rereads that of Monsigny.[10] The public goes to exhibitions by M. Vuillard or M. Maurice Denis, whereas the latter go to the Louvre.) This stems doubtless from the fact that the contemporary ideas which writers and artists of originality make accessible and desirable to the public, are to some extent so much part of them that they are more easily diverted by different ideas. It asks a greater effort of them, to go to where these are, and so gives them more pleasure; we always like to be taken out of ourselves a little, to travel, when we read.

But there is another cause to which, finally, I would rather ascribe this predilection in great minds for old works.[11] Which is that, unlike contemporary works, they do not only have for us the beauty which the mind that created them was able to put into them. They receive another beauty, more affecting still, from the fact that their substance, I mean the language in which they were written, is like a mirror of life. Something of the happiness one feels walking in a town like Beaune, whose fifteenth-century hospice has been preserved intact, with its well, its wash-house, the painted panels of its wooden ceiling,

the tall gabled roof, pierced by dormer windows sur-
mounted by frail finials of beaten lead (all the things that
an age left behind there as it were when it vanished, all the
things that were its alone since none of the ages which
followed saw anything similar arise), one feels something
of that happiness again as one wanders in the midst of a
tragedy by Racine or a volume of Saint-Simon. For these
contain all the lovely suppressed forms of a language
that preserve the memory of usages or ways of feeling
which no longer exist, persistent traces of the past unlike
anything in the present and whose colours time alone,
as it passed over them, has been able further to enhance.

A tragedy by Racine or a volume of Saint-Simon's
memoirs resemble beautiful objects which are no longer
made. The language from which they have been
sculpted, by great artists, with a freedom which shows
off its mellowness and brings out its native vigour, affects
us like the sight of certain marbles, uncommon today,
which were used by the workmen of old. No doubt in
this old building or that the stone has faithfully preserved
the sculptor's thought, but also, thanks to the sculptor,
the stone itself, of a kind unknown today, has been
preserved for us, dressed in all the colours he was able
to extract from it, to show off and to harmonize. It
is very much the living syntax of seventeenth-century
France – and in it customs and a way of thinking that
have vanished – which we love to discover in the poetry
of Racine. It is the actual forms of this syntax, laid bare,
reverenced, embellished by his very free yet very delicate
chisel, which move us in those turns of phrase so col-
loquial as to be both strange and daring,[12] whose abrupt

pattern we can see, in the gentlest and tenderest of passages, pass swiftly by like an arrow or turn back in lovely, broken lines. It is these obsolete forms drawn from the life of the past itself which we go to visit in the work of Racine as in some ancient yet still intact citadel. Before them we feel the same emotion as before those architectural forms, likewise suppressed, which we can now admire only in the rare and magnificent examples of them bequeathed to us by the past which fashioned them: such as old town walls, keeps and towers, or the baptisteries of churches; such as, next to the cloister, or beneath the charnel-house of the Aître, the little burial ground where, beneath its butterflies and its flowers, the funerary Fountain and the Lantern of the Dead stand forgotten in the sun.

Furthermore, it is not only the phrases themselves that trace for us the forms of the ancient soul. Between the phrases – I am thinking of those books of antiquity which were originally recited, – in the interval which separates them, there is still contained today, as in some inviolate hypogeum, filling their interstices, a silence many centuries old. Often, in St Luke's Gospel, when I come upon the 'colons' which punctuate it before each of the almost canticle-like passages with which it is strewn,[13] I have heard the silence of the worshipper who has just stopped from reading out loud so as to intone the verses following,[14] like a psalm reminding him of the older psalms in the Bible. This silence still filled the pause in the sentence which, having been split into two so as to enclose it, had preserved its shape; and more than once, as I was reading, it brought to me the scent of a rose which the breeze entering by the open window had spread through the upper room where the Gathering was being held and which had not evaporated in almost two thousand years. *The Divine Comedy* or the plays of Shakespeare also give one an impression of contemplating something of the past, inserted into the present moment; that very uplifting impression which makes certain 'days of reading' resemble days spent strolling in Venice, on the Piazzetta for example, where before you, in their half unreal colours of objects at once a few paces and many centuries distant, you have the twin columns of pink and grey granite bearing on their capitals, the one the lion of St Mark and the other St Theodore trampling on the crocodile; these two beautiful and slender foreigners came once from the East, across the sea that is breaking at their feet; uncomprehending of the remarks exchanged around them, they continue to live out their twelfth-century days amidst the crowds of today, on that public square where, close beside you, there still gleams their remote and distracted smile.

Notes

1. I have to admit that a certain use of the imperfect indicative – that cruel tense which portrays life to us as something both ephemeral and passive, and which, in the very act of retracing our actions, reduces them to an illusion, annihilating them in the past without, unlike the perfect, leaving us with the consolation of activity – has remained for me an inexhaustible source of mysterious sadness. Even today I can have been reflecting calmly on death

for hours on end; but I only have to open a volume of Sainte-Beuve's *Lundis* and light, for example, upon these words of Lamartine's (they concern Mme d'Albany). 'Nothing about her at that time recalled [*rappelait*] . . . She was [*c'était*] a small woman whose figure had somewhat collapsed beneath her weight and lost, etc.,' to feel myself at once invaded by the profoundest melancholy. In novels the author's intention of making us suffer is so obvious that we brace ourselves rather better.

2.   One can try this, in a roundabout way, with books which are not pure imagination but have a substratum of history. Balzac, for example, whose work is in a sense impure, being a mixture of thought and of a reality insufficiently transformed, sometimes lends himself particularly well to being read in this way. He has at any rate found the most admirable of 'historical readers' in M. Albert Sorel, who has written matchless essays on *Une Ténébreuse affaire* and *L'Envers de l'histoire contemporaine*. How well reading, indeed, an enjoyment at once ardent and sedate, seems to suit M. Sorel, with his inquiring spirit and his calm, powerful body, reading, in the course of which the countless sensations of poetry and of a vague contentment that wing cheerfully up from the depths of our well-being come to create a pleasure as sweet and as golden as honey around the reader's reverie. It is not only with semi-historical works, either, that M. Sorel has perfected this art of encompassing so many powerful and original reflections within a single reading. I shall always remember – and with such gratitude – that my study of *The Bible of Amiens* was the subject of perhaps the most powerful pages he has ever written.

3.   In point of fact this sentence is not to be found in *Le Capitaine Fracasse*, at least in this form. Instead of 'so it

appears from the *Odyssey* of Homerus, the Grecian poet,'
we have simply 'according to Homerus'. But since the
expressions 'it appears from Homerus' and 'it appears
from the *Odyssey*', to be found elsewhere in the book,
gave me the same degree of delight, I have permitted
myself, so that the example might be more striking for
my readers, to fuse all these beauties into one, now that,
truth to tell, I no longer feel a religious veneration for
them. Elsewhere in *Le Capitaine Fracasse*, Homerus is
again described as a Grecian poet, and I do not doubt but
that this too enchanted me. All the same I am no longer
capable of recovering these forgotten joys with sufficient
accuracy to be sure that I have not gone too far and
overstepped the mark in amassing so many wonderful
things in a single sentence! I do not think so, however.
And I reflect to my regret that the exhilaration with which
I used to repeat that sentence from *Le Capitaine Fracasse*
to the irises and the periwinkles overhanging the river-
bank, as I trod the gravel of the path, would have been
more delightful still had I been able to find in a single
sentence of Gautier's so many of the charms which my
own artifice has gathered here today, though without,
alas, affording me any pleasure.

4.   The germ of it is there I sense in Fontanes, of whom
Sainte-Beuve said: 'This epicurean side was very strong in
him . . . but for these rather materialistic habits, Fontanes,
with his talent, would have produced much more . . . and
more lasting works.' Note that the impotent man always
claims not to be so. Fontanes says:

> If they are to be believed I waste my time,
> They alone do honour to the century

and assures us of his own industry.

Coleridge's is a more pathological case still. 'No man of his time, or perhaps of any other time,' says Carpenter (quoted by M. Ribot in his fine book on *Diseases of the Will*), 'combined better than Coleridge the power of reasoning of the philosopher with the imagination of the poet, etc. And yet no one gifted with such remarkable talents has ever made so little of them: the great defect of his character was a lack of willpower to turn his natural gifts to advantage, so that although he always had gigantic projects floating in his brain, he never made a serious effort to execute a single one of them. Thus, from the outset of his career, he found a generous bookseller who promised him thirty guineas for the poems he had been reciting, etc. He preferred to come begging each week without supplying a single line of the poem he needed only to write down to be set free.'

5. I have no need to say that it would be pointless to look for this convent near Utrecht and that this whole passage is pure imagination. It was suggested to me however by the following lines in M. Léon Séché's book on Sainte-Beuve: 'He (Sainte-Beuve) took it into his head one day, while he was at Liège, to get in touch with the little church in Utrecht. It was quite late but Utrecht was a good long way from Paris and I do not know whether *Volupté* would have sufficed to open the doors to the archives in Amersfoort wide to him. I rather doubt it, because even after the first two volumes of his *Port-Royal*, the devout scholar who then had charge of these archives, etc. With difficulty Sainte-Beuve obtained permission from the good M. Karsten to glance inside certain cardboard boxes . . . Open the second edition of *Port-Royal* and you will find the gratitude which Sainte-Beuve ex-

pressed to M. Karsten.' As for the details of the journey, all of them rely on actual impressions. I do not know whether one goes through Dordrecht to get to Utrecht, but I have described it just as I saw it. It was when going to Vollendam, and not to Utrecht, that I travelled by passenger barge, amongst the reeds. The canal which I have set in Utrecht is in Delft. It was in the Hôpital of Beaune that I saw a Van der Weyden and nuns of an order which came, I believe, from Flanders, and who still wear the same headdresses, not as in the Roger van der Weyden but as in other paintings I saw in Holland.

6. Pure snobbery is more innocent. To take pleasure in someone's company because he had an ancestor at the Crusades, that is vanity, intelligence does not enter into it. But to take pleasure in someone's company because the name of his grandfather recurs frequently in Alfred de Vigny or in Chateaubriand, or (a truly irresistible attraction for me, I must confess) who has her family coat-of-arms (the woman in question is richly deserving of admiration without this) in the great rose-window of Notre-Dame in Amiens, that is where the intellectual sin begins. I have anyway analysed this at too great a length elsewhere, although I have much left to say on the matter, to need to insist on it further here.

7. I am told that he became the celebrated Admiral de Tinan, father of Mme Pochet de Tinan, whose name artists still hold dear, and the grandfather of the dashing cavalry officer. It was he also, I believe, who was in charge of supplies and communications between Francis II and the Queen of Naples before Gaeta (see Pierre de la Gorce's *Histoire du Second Empire*).

8. True distinction, moreover, always feigns to be addressing itself only to persons of distinction who know the same

usages, it does not 'explain'. A book by Anatole France hints at a mass of erudite knowledge, and contains constant allusions that the masses will overlook but which, independently of its other beauties, constitute its incomparable nobility.

9. This is no doubt why often, when a great writer turns critic, he talks a lot about the available editions of old works, and very little about contemporary books. Example, the *Lundis* of Sainte-Beuve and Anatole France's *Vie littéraire*. But whereas M. Anatole France is a wonderful judge of his contemporaries, it may be said that Sainte-Beuve misinterpreted all the great writers of his own day. And let it not be objected that he was blinded by personal animosities. After, unbelievably, having disparaged the novelist in Stendhal, by way of compensation he extols the modesty and tactful dealings of the man, as if there were nothing else to be said in his favour! This blindness in Sainte-Beuve, where his own time was concerned, contrasts oddly with his pretensions to clear-sightedness and to prescience. 'Everyone is adept,' he says in *Chateaubriand et son groupe littéraire*, 'at pronouncing on Racine and Bossuet . . . But the sagaciousness of the judge and the perspicacity of the critic prove themselves above all on new writings as yet untried by the public. To judge at first sight, to divine, to lead the way, that is the gift of the critic. How few possess it.'

10. And, vice versa, the classics have had no better commentators than the 'Romantics'. The Romantics alone indeed know how to read classical works, because they read them as they were written, romantically, because to read a poet or a prose writer properly, one has oneself to be, not a scholar, but a poet or a prose writer. This is true for the least 'Romantic' of works. It was not the professors

of rhetoric who drew our attention to Boileau's beautiful lines, but Victor Hugo:

> *Et dans quatre mouchoirs de sa beauté salis*
> *Envoie au blanchissuer ses roses et ses lys.*

> And in four handkerchiefs soiled by her beauty
> Sends to the laundryman her roses and her lilies.

Or M. Anatole France:

> *L'ignorance et l'erreur à ses naissantes pièces*
> *En habits de marquis, en robes de comtesse.*

> Ignorance and error in his newborn plays
> In a marquis's clothes, in a countess's robes.

The latest issue of *La Renaissance latine* (15 May 1905) has enabled me, as I was correcting my proofs, to extend this observation to the fine arts, by means of a fresh example. This shows M. Rodin, indeed (in an article by M. Mauclair), to be the true commentator on Greek statuary.

11. A predilection which they themselves generally believe to be fortuitous: they assume that the best books merely chance to have been written by ancient authors; and this may happen no doubt, because the old books which we read have been selected from the past as a whole, so vast compared with the modern age. But an in a sense accidental reason can not suffice to explain an attitude of mind so general.

12. I think for example that the charm normally found in these lines from *Andromaque*:

Pourquoi l'assassiner? Qu'a-t-il fait? A quel titre?
Qui te l'a dit?

Why murder him? What has he done? On what grounds?
Who told you?

comes precisely from the fact that the usual syntactical
links have been deliberately broken. 'On what grounds?'
relates not to the 'What has he done' immediately preceding, but to 'Why murder him?' And 'Who told you?' also
relates to 'murder' (Recalling another line in *Andromaque*:
'Who told you, my Lord, that he despises me?' one
might imagine that 'Who told you?' stands for 'Who told
you to murder him?'). Zigzags in the expression (the
recurring, broken line I speak of above) which do not fail
to obscure the sense somewhat, so that I have heard a
great actress, more concerned for the clarity of the speech
than the accuracy of the prosody, say straight out: 'Why
murder him? On what grounds? What has he done?'
Racine's most celebrated lines are so in point of fact
because we are charmed when some bold colloquialism
is thus thrown like an impetuous bridge between two
mellow river-banks. 'Je t'aimais inconstant, *qu'aurais-je
fait* fidèle.' [I was inconstant and loved you, what would
I have done had I been true.] And what pleasure they
give, these splendid encounters with expressions whose
almost vulgar simplicity lends to their meaning, as to
certain of Mantegna's faces, so sweet a fullness, such
lovely colours:

> *Et dans un fol amour ma jeunesse* embarquée . . .
> And on a mad love my youth embarked

Réunissons trois coeurs qui n'ont pu s'accorder.
Let us unite three hearts unable to agree.

This is why it is right to read classical authors in the text and not be satisfied with extracts. The famous passages of writers are often those where this intimate contexture of their language is disguised by the beauty – almost universal in character – of the extract. I do not believe that the essence peculiar to the music of Gluck reveals itself in any one of his sublime arias so much as in certain cadences of his recitative, where the harmony is like the actual sound of the voice of his genius as it drops on an involuntary intonation on which is stamped all of his artless gravity and distinction, each time one hears him catch his breath so to speak. Anyone who has seen photographs of St Mark's in Venice may imagine (but I speak only of the outside of that monument) that he has some idea of that domed church, whereas it is only as you approach the mottled curtain of its cheerful columns, until you can touch them with your hand, only when you see the strange and solemn power that has wreathed the foliage or made birds to perch in those capitals, distinguishable only from close to, only when you have had an impression from the square itself of this low-set building, and the full length of its façade, with its flowered masts and festival decoration, its 'exhibition-hall' look, that you feel its true and complex individuality burst forth from these significant yet subsidiary features which no photograph can capture.

13. 'And Mary said: "My soul doth magnify the Lord and my spirit hath rejoiced in God my Saviour," etc. Zacharias her father was filled with the Holy Ghost and prophesied saying: "Blessed be the Lord, God of Israel for that he has

redeemed," etc. "He took him up in his arms, blessed God and said, 'Lord, now lettest thou thy servant depart in peace.'"'

14. In truth there is no positive evidence enabling me to affirm that when reading like this the reciter chanted the sort of psalms which St Luke has inserted into his gospel. But it seems to me to come out sufficiently strongly from a comparison of various passages in Renan and notably in St Paul, the Apostles, Marcus Aurelius, etc.

Days of Reading (II)

You have no doubt read the *Memoirs* of the Countess de Boigne. There are 'so many people ill' at the moment, that books are finding readers, even female ones. When one is unable to go out and pay calls, one would rather receive them no doubt than read. But 'in these days of epidemics' even the calls one receives are not without danger. There is the lady who pauses for a moment – just for a moment – in the doorway, where she puts a frame round her threat, to call to you: 'You're not afraid of mumps or scarlet fever? I must warn you that my daughter and my grandchildren have got them. Can I come in?'; and comes in without waiting for a reply. There is another lady, less candid, who pulls out her watch: 'I must be off home; my three daughters have got measles; I go from one to the other; my English girl has been in bed since yesterday with a high fever, and I'm very much afraid it may be my turn to be caught, because I felt off colour when I got up. But I had to make the big effort to come and see you . . .'

So one prefers not to entertain too much and since one cannot be always telephoning, one reads. One reads only as an absolutely last resort. First, we do a lot of telephoning. And, since we are children who play with the sacred powers unawed by their mystery, we find merely with the telephone that 'it is convenient', or

rather, since we are spoilt children, that 'it is not convenient' and fill *Le Figaro* with our complaints, finding
this wonderful fairy-land still not fast enough in its trans-
formations, when several minutes may sometimes elapse
indeed before there appears beside us, invisible yet present, the friend to whom we had desired to speak and
who, though still at her table, in the far-off town where
she lives, beneath skies different from ours, in weather
not as it is here, in the midst of circumstances and
pre-occupations of which we know nothing but of which
she is about to tell us, finds herself suddenly transported
a hundred miles away (herself, and the whole ambience
in which she remains immersed), against our ear, at a
moment ordained by our own whim. And we are like
the character in the fairy-tale who, this being what he
has wished for, is shown his betrothed by a wizard, with
a magical clarity, in the act of looking through a book,
or shedding tears, or picking flowers, right beside him,
yet in the place where she then is, far away.

For this miracle to be renewed for us, we have only to
put our lips to the magic planchette-board and summon –
for quite some time on occasions, I will agree – the
vigilant Virgins whose voices we hear every day without
ever knowing their faces and who are our guardian
angels in that vertiginous darkness whose gates they
watch over jealously, the Omnipotent ones thanks to
whom the faces of the absent loom up beside us without
our being allowed to see them; we have only to summon
these Danaids of the Invisible who empty, recharge and
hand on to one another unceasingly the dark urns of
sounds, the jealous Furies who, as we murmur a confi-

dence to a woman friend, call out to us ironically: 'I'm on the line,' at a moment when we were hoping no one could hear us, the irate servants of the Mystery, the implacable Divinities, the Damsels of the telephone! And the instant their summons has sounded in the night full of apparitions to which our ears alone are opened, a faint sound, an abstract sound – of distance being suppressed – and the voice of our friend is addressing us.

If at that moment the singing of a passer-by, the horn of a bicyclist or a distant regimental band should enter by the window to importune her as she is speaking to us, they ring out just as distinctly for us (as if to prove that it is indeed she who is beside us, with everything that surrounds her at that moment, that is striking her ear and distracting her attention) – truthful details, nothing to do with the subject, useless in themselves, but all the more necessary as revealing to us the full evidence of the miracle – prosaic and charming elements of local colour, descriptive of the provincial street and roadway to be seen from her house, such as a poet chooses when he wants to bring a character alive and evokes his milieu.

It is she, it is her voice which is speaking to us, which is there. But how far away it is! How many times have I been able to listen to it without anguish, as if, faced by the impossibility of seeing, without long hours of travelling, the person whose voice was so close to my ear, I sensed more clearly how disappointing this semblance of the sweetest proximity is and how far distant we may be from the things we love at the moment when it seems we need only stretch out our hand to detain them. A real presence – this voice so close – in an effective separation. But an anticipation also of an everlasting separation. Very often, listening to it in this fashion, unable to see the person who was speaking to me from so far away, her voice seemed to be crying out from the depths from which one does not reascend, and I experienced the anxiety that would one day seize hold of me, when a voice returned to me thus, alone no longer dependent on a body I should never set eyes on again, to murmur in my ear words I would like to have been able to embrace as they passed on lips that are forever dust.

I was saying that before making up our minds to read, we try to keep on conversing, to telephone, we ask for number after number. But sometimes the Daughters of the Night, the Messengers of the Word, the faceless Goddesses, the capricious Guardians cannot or will not open the gates of the Invisible to us, the Mystery we solicit remains deaf, the venerable inventor of printing and the young prince who was both a lover of Impressionist painting and a motorist – Gutenberg and Wagram! [two Parisian telephone exchanges] – upon whom they call tirelessly, leave their supplications unanswered; then, since we cannot pay calls, since we do not wish to receive them, since the damsels of the telephone cannot connect us, we resign ourselves to being silent, we read.

In only a few weeks' time we shall be able to read the new volume of poetry by Mme de Noailles, *Les Eblouissements* (I do not know whether it will keep that title), superior even to those books of genius, *Le Coeur innombrable* and *L'Ombre des jours*, the equal in fact, it seems to me, of the *Feuilles d'automne* or the *Fleurs du mal*. Meanwhile, we might read the pure and exquisite

Margaret Ogilvy de Barrie, wonderfully well translated by R. d'Humières, which is simply the life of a peasant woman told by a poet, her son. But no; the moment we resign ourselves to reading, we choose for preference books like the *Memoirs* of Mme de Boigne, books which give us the illusion of continuing to pay calls, calls on people we had not been able to visit before because we were not yet born under Louis XVI, but who are not so very different as it happens from the people whom you know because almost all of them bear the same names as they do, their descendants and your friends who, by a touching courtesy towards your ailing memory, have kept the same first names and are still called: Odon, Ghislain, Nivelon, Victurnien, Josselin, Léonor, Artus, Tucdual, Adhéaume or Raynulphe. Fine baptismal names moreover, which one would do wrong to smile at; they come from a past so profound that in their unwonted lustre they seem to sparkle mysteriously, like those names of prophets and saints inscribed in brief in the stained-glass of our cathedrals. Does Jehan itself, although more like one of today's names, not appear inevitably as if traced in Gothic characters in a Book of Hours by a brush dipped in purple, ultramarine or azure? Faced with such names, the common people would perhaps repeat the Montmartre song:

> Bragance, on le connaît ct'oiseau-là;
> Faut-il que son orgueil soye profonde
> Pour s'être f . . . u un nom comme ça!
> Peut donc pas s'appeler comme tout le monde!

Bragance, we know that character;
He must be really big-headed
To have got himself a f . . . ing name like that!
Couldn't he have a name like everyone else!

But the poet, if he is sincere, does not share in such merriment but, with his eyes fixed on the past that such names disclose to him, will reply with Verlaine:

Je vois, j'entends beaucoup de choses
Dans son nom Carlovingien.

I see, I hear many things
In his Carolingian name.

An enormous past perhaps. I should like to think that these names, so few examples of which have come down to us, thanks to the attachment to tradition of certain families, were in the old days very common names – the names of villeins as well as noblemen – so that, through the naive colours of the magic-lantern slides that such names offer us, it is not only the mighty lord with the blue beard or Sister Anne in her tower that we can see, but also the peasant bent over the ripening meadow or the men-at-arms riding along dusty thirteenth-century roads.

Very often no doubt the medieval impression their names give off does not survive an acquaintance with those who bear them and who have neither preserved nor understood their poetry; but can we reasonably ask of human beings that they should show themselves worthy of their names when the most beautiful things have so much difficulty in living up to theirs, when there is no landscape, no city, no river the sight of which can assuage the dreamlike desire its name had given birth to in us? The sensible thing would be to replace all our society connections and many journeys by a reading of the Almanach de Gotha or the railway timetable . . .

What is moving about Memoirs from the end of the eighteenth century and the beginning of the nineteenth, like those of the Countess de Boigne, is that they lend to the contemporary age, to our own days that are lived without beauty, a rather noble, rather melancholy perspective, by making them as it were into the foreground of History. They enable us to pass easily from the persons whom we have met with in life – or whom our parents have known – to the parents of those persons, who themselves, as authors or as characters in these Memoirs, may have witnessed the Revolution and seen Marie-Antoinette go by. So that the people whom we may have been able to glimpse or to know – the people we have seen with our own eyes – are like those life-size wax models in the foreground of panoramas, treading on real grass and holding up a cane bought from a shop, who seem still to be part of the crowd that is gazing at them and lead us gradually to the painted backcloth, to which, thanks to skilfully contrived transitions, they lend the three-dimensional appearance of life and reality. This Mme de Boigne then, born a d'Osmond and brought up, so she tells us, on the laps of Louis XVI and Marie-Antoinette, as an adolescent I very often saw her niece at balls, the old Duchess de Maillé, née d'Osmond, over eighty yet still splendid beneath the grey hair brushed upwards from her forehead which put one in mind of the bob-wigs worn by presidents in the High Court. And I recall that my parents very often dined with Mme de Boigne's nephew, M. d'Osmond, for whom she wrote these Memoirs and whose photograph I found among their papers, together with many letters he had addressed to them. So that my own earliest memories of balls, which hang by a thread from the for me somewhat less distinct yet still very real accounts of my parents, are connected by an already almost immaterial link to the memories which Mme de Boigne had preserved and which she recounts to us of the earliest entertainments at which she was present; all of which weaves a tissue of frivolities, yet a poetic one, for it ends as the stuff of dreams, a slender bridge thrown between the present and an already distant past, and which joins life to history, making history more alive and life almost historical.

Here I am, alas, at the third column of the newspaper and I have not yet begun my article even. It was to have been called. 'Snobbery and Posterity', but I am not going to be able to leave it with that title since I have filled the entire space reserved for me without saying a single word to you as yet about either Snobbery or Posterity, two persons whom you no doubt thought would never be called upon to meet, for the greater good fortune of the second, and on the topic of whom I was intending to subject you to a few reflections inspired by reading the *Memoirs* of Mme de Boigne. That must wait until next time. And if then one of those phantoms that interpose themselves ceaselessly between my mind and its object, as happens in dreams, should again come to solicit my attention and distract it from what I have to say to you, I shall thrust it aside just as Ulysses thrust aside with his sword the shades that crowded round him imploring him for a human form or for burial.

Today I have been unable to resist the appeal of these visions that I could see floating halfway down, in the transparency of my mind. And I have attempted without success what the master glassmaker so often achieved when he transported and fixed his dreams, at the very distance at which they had appeared to him, between two waters clouded by dark, pink reflections, in a translucid substance in which at times a fitful ray of light, coming from its heart, might have made them think that they were still at play inside a living mind. Like the Nereids which the sculptor of antiquity had snatched from the sea but who could still believe themselves to be immersed in it as they swam between the marble waves of the bas-relief that figured it. I was wrong. It will not happen again. Next time I shall talk to you of snobbery and posterity, without digressing. And should some unto-ward idea, some indiscreet fancy seek to meddle in what is none of its business and threaten once more to interrupt us, I shall at once beg it to let us be: 'We are talking, do not cut us off, mademoiselle!'

From *The Method of Sainte-Beuve*
(extracts)

[. . .]

Thus it seems to me that I would have things that have
their importance perhaps to say about Sainte-Beuve, and
presently much more in connection with him than about
him, that by showing where he sinned, in my view, both
as writer and as critic, I should perhaps come to say
some things about which I have often thought as to what
criticism should be and what art is. In passing, and in his
connection, as he does so often, I shall use him as the
excuse for talking about certain forms of life . . .

[. . .]

For the definition and eulogizing of Sainte-Beuve's
method I have looked to the article by M. Paul Bourget,
because the definition was short and the eulogy authori-
tative. I could have cited twenty other critics. To have
written the natural history of minds, to have looked to
the biography of the man, to the history of his family, to
all his peculiarities, for an understanding of his work and
the nature of his genius, that is what everyone recognizes
to have been his originality, and what he recognized
himself, in which moreover he was right. Taine himself,
who dreamt of a more systematic and better codified

natural history of men's minds and with whom as it happens Sainte-Beuve did not agree over questions of race, says no differently in his eulogy of Sainte-Beuve: 'M. Sainte-Beuve's method is no less valuable than his work. In this he was a pioneer. He imported into moral history the procedures of natural history.'

[. . .]

Now, in art there are no initiators or precursors (at least in the scientific sense). Everything is in the individual, each individual starts the artistic or literary endeavour over again, on his own account; the works of his predecessors do not constitute, unlike in science, an acquired truth from which he who follows after may profit. A writer of genius today has it all to do. He is not much further advanced than Homer.

But those philosophers who have been unable to find what is real and independent of all science in art have been forced to imagine art, criticism, etc., to themselves as sciences in which the predecessor is necessarily less far advanced than whoever follows after him.

But why trouble anyway to name all those who see in this the originality and excellence of Sainte-Beuve's method? One need only let him speak for himself.

'For me,' said Sainte-Beuve, 'literature is not distinct or at any rate separable from the rest of the man and of his organization . . . We cannot go about it in too many different ways or from too many different angles if we are to get to know a man, something more than a pure intelligence, that is. Until such time as one has put to oneself a certain number of questions about an author, and has answered them, be it only to oneself alone and under one's breath, one cannot be sure of having grasped him entire, even though the questions may seem quite foreign to the nature of his writings: What were his religious ideas? How did the spectacle of nature affect him? How did he behave in the matter of women, of money? Was he rich, poor; what was his diet, his daily routine? What was his vice or his weakness? None of the answers to these questions is irrelevant if we are to judge the author of a book or the book itself, provided that book is not a treatise on pure geometry, if it is a work of literature above all, one, that is, which brings in everything, etc.' This method which he applied instinctively all his life and in which towards the end he saw the first outlines of a sort of literary botany . . .

Sainte-Beuve's is not a profound oeuvre. The famous method which in fact, according to Taine, to M. Paul Bourget and to so many others, made him the peerless master of nineteenth-century criticism – that method which consists of not separating the man from the work, of considering that it is not irrelevant if we are to judge the author of a book, unless the book is 'a treatise on pure geometry', to have first answered questions which seem quite foreign to his work (how did he behave . . .), to surround oneself with all the possible facts about a writer, to collate his correspondence, to question the people who knew him, talking with them if they are still alive, reading what they may have written about him if they are dead – such a method fails to recognize what any more than merely superficial acquaintance with ourselves teaches us: that a book is the product of a self other than that which we display in our habits, in company, in our vices. If we want to try and understand this self, it is deep inside us, by trying to recreate it within us, that we may succeed. This is an effort of the heart from which nothing can absolve us. It is a truth every bit of which we have to create and . . . It is too easy to suppose that it will arrive one fine morning among our mail, in the form of an unpublished letter imparted to us by a librarian friend, or that we shall gather it from the lips of someone who knew the author well. Speaking of the great admiration aroused in several writers of the new generation by the work of Stendhal [Henri Beyle], Sainte-Beuve says: 'May they permit me to tell them, that if we are clearly to judge that rather complicated mind and not exaggerate at all in any direction, I shall always come back for preference, independently of my own impressions and memories, to what those who knew him in his prime and when he was starting out have to say about him, to M. Mérimée, to M. Ampère, to what Jacquemont would have to tell me about him were he still alive, to those, in short, who saw and savoured much of him in his earlier version.'

Why so? How does the fact of having been a friend of Stendhal make us better able to judge him? On the contrary, it would probably be a serious hindrance. For such intimates the self which produces the works is obscured by the other self, which may be very inferior to the outward self of many other men. The best proof of which moreover is that, having known Stendhal, and having collected up all the facts he could from 'M. Mérimée' and 'M. Ampère', having equipped himself, in short, with everything which, according to him, enables a critic to judge a book more accurately, Sainte-Beuve judged Stendhal in the following manner: 'I have just reread, or tried to, the novels of Stendhal; they are frankly detestable.'

[. . .]

He ends with these two gems: 'Criticize Beyle's novels with some candour though I may, I am far from censuring him for having written them . . . His novels are what they may be, but they are not vulgar. They are like his criticism, for the use chiefly of those who write them . . .' And the concluding words of the article: 'Beyle had a fundamental straightforwardness and reliability in his personal dealings which we must never forget to acknowledge once we have said our piece about him.' A good fellow, Beyle, all things considered. To reach which conclusion it was perhaps scarcely worth the trouble of meeting M. Mérimée so often at dinner or at the Academy, or 'setting M. Ampère talking' so much, and once having read it one is less anxious than Sainte-Beuve was at the thought of the new generations to come.

[. . .]

At no time does Sainte-Beuve seem to have grasped what is peculiar to inspiration or the activity of writing, and what marks it off totally from the occupations of other men and the other occupations of the writer. He drew no dividing line between the occupation of writing, in which, in solitude and suppressing those words which belong as much to others as to ourselves, and with which, even when alone, we judge things without being ourselves, we come face to face once more with our selves, and seek to hear and to render the true sound of our hearts – and conversation!

It is only the deceptive appearance of the image here which lends something vaguer and more external to the writer's craft and something deeper and more contemplative to sociability. In actual fact what one gives to the public is what one has written when alone, for oneself, it is very much the work of one's self . . . What one gives to sociability, that is to conversation (however refined it may be, and the most refined is the worst of all, because it falsifies our spiritual life by associating itself to it: Flaubert's conversations with his niece or with the clockmaker are without risk) or to those productions intended for one's intimates, that is to say reduced so as to appeal to a few and which are barely more than written conversation, is the work of a far more external self, not of the deep self which is only to be found by disregarding other people and the self that knows other people, the self that has been waiting while one was with others, which one feels clearly to be the only real self, for which alone artists end by living, like a god whom they leave less and less and to whom they have sacrificed a life that serves only to do him honour.

[. . .]

And not having seen the gulf that separates the writer from the society man, not having understood that the writer's self shows itself only in his books, that he only shows society men (even those society men that other writers are, when in society, who only become writers again once on their own) a society man like themselves, he was to launch that famous method which, according to Taine, Bourget and so many others, is his claim to fame, and which consists, in order to understand a poet or writer, in questioning avidly those who knew him, who frequented him, who may be able to tell us how he behaved in the matter of women, etc., that is, on all those very points where the poet's true self is not involved.

[...]

Just as we find Sainte-Beuve believing that the salon life which he enjoyed was indispensable to literature, and projecting it across the centuries, here to the court of Louis XIV, there to the select circle of the Directory, so ... In point of fact this seven-days-a-week creator, who often did not rest even on Sundays and who received his wages of fame on Mondays from the pleasure he gave to good judges and the knocks he inflicted on the unkind ones, saw all of literature as a sort of *Lundis* which may perhaps be reread but which have had to be written in their own time heedful of the opinion of the good judges, in order to please and not relying too much on posterity. He sees literature under the category of time. [...] Literature seems to him to be of its period, to be worth what the person was worth. In sum, it is better to play a major role in politics and not to write than to be a political malcontent and write a book on morality ...

etc. He was not like Emerson, therefore, who said that we must hitch our wagon to a star. He tries to hitch his to the most contingent thing of all, to politics.

[. . .]

I wonder at times whether what is still best in Sainte-Beuve is not his poetry. There the intellectual games have ceased. He no longer comes at things obliquely, with endless clevernesses and trickery. The magic and infernal circle has been broken. In ceasing to speak in prose he ceases to tell lies, as if the constant mendacity of his thought stemmed in his case from his contrived skill in expression. Just as a student, forced to translate his thoughts into Latin, is forced to lay them bare, so Sainte-Beuve finds himself for the first time in the presence of reality and receives a direct sense of it. [. . .] Of him, of the deep, unconscious, personal self there is hardly anything bar the clumsiness. That recurs frequently, as nature will. But the trifling thing, the trifling yet also delightful and sincere thing that is his poetry, that skilful and at times successful attempt to express the purity of love, the sadness of late afternoons in large towns, the magic of memory, the emotion of reading, the melancholy of an unbelieving old age, demonstrates – because one feels that it is the only real thing about him – the lack of significance in his vast, marvellous, ebullient oeuvre as a critic – for all these marvels come down to this. Mere appearance, the *Lundis*. The reality, this handful of poems. The poems of a critic, they it is out of all his writings that tip eternity's scales.

Swann *Explained by Proust*
[Published November 1913]

'I am publishing only one volume, *Du côté de chez Swann*, of a novel whose general title will be *A la recherche du temps perdu*. I would like to have brought the whole of it out at once; but works in several volumes are no longer being published. I am like someone who has a tapestry too large for present-day apartments, and who has been obliged to cut it up.

'Young writers, with whom I am otherwise in sympathy, advocate on the contrary a succinct plot with few characters. That is not my conception of the novel. How to put it to you? You know that there is plane geometry and solid geometry. Well, for me, the novel is not only plane psychology, but psychology in time. I have attempted to isolate the invisible substance of time, but to do that the experiment had to be able to be long-lasting. I hope that at the end of my book, some minor social event of no importance, some marriage between two persons who in the first volume belong to very different worlds, will indicate that time has passed and will take on the beauty of certain patinated leadwork at Versailles, which time has encased in an emerald sheath.

'Then, like a town which, as the train follows a curve in the track, appears now on our right hand and now on our left, the various aspects that a single character has taken on in someone else's eyes, to the extent of being like different and successive characters, will convey – but only by this – the sensation of time having elapsed. Particular characters will later reveal themselves as different from what they are in the present volume, and different from what they will be believed to be, as very often happens in life for that matter.

'It is not only the same characters who will reappear in the course of the work under different aspects, as in certain cycles by Balzac, but,' M. Proust tells us, 'certain profound, almost unconscious impressions within a single character.

'From this point of view,' M. Proust goes on, 'my book would perhaps be like an attempt at a sequence of "Novels of the Unconscious"; I would not be at all ashamed to say "Bergsonian novels" if I believed that, for it happens in every age that literature attempts to attach itself – *post hoc*, of course – to the prevailing philosophy. But that would not be accurate, for my work is dominated by the distinction between involuntary and voluntary memory, a distinction which not only does not appear in M. Bergson's philosophy but is even contradicted by it.'

'How do you substantiate this distinction?'

'For me, voluntary memory, which is above all a memory of the intellect and of the eyes, gives us only facets of the past that have no truth; but should a smell or a taste, met with again in quite different circumstances, reawaken the past in us, in spite of ourselves, we sense how different that past was from what we thought we had remembered, our voluntary memory having painted it, like a bad painter, in false colours. Already, in this first volume, you will find the character who tells the story and who says "I" (who is not me) suddenly recovering years, gardens, people he has forgotten, in the taste of a mouthful of tea in which he has soaked a bit of madeleine; he could have remembered them no doubt, but without their colour or their charm; I have been able to make him say that, as in that little Japanese game where you soak flimsy bits of paper which, the moment you immerse them in the bowl, spread out and writhe and turn into flowers and characters, all the flowers in his garden, and the water-lilies of the Vivonne, and the good people of the village and their little houses and the church, and the whole of Combray and its surroundings, whatever can take on shape and solidity, has emerged, town and gardens, out of his cup of tea.

'You see, I believe that it is really only to involuntary memories that the artist should go for the raw material of his work. First, precisely because they are involuntary and take shape of their own accord, drawn by the resemblance of some identical moment, they alone bear the hallmark of authenticity. Then, they bring things back to us in exact proportions of memory and oblivion. And finally, since they give us to enjoy the same sensation in quite other circumstances, they release it from all contingency, they give us its extratemporal essence, which is the very content of good style, that general and necessary truth that the beauty of a style alone can reveal.

'If I permit myself to rationalize about my book like this,' M. Proust continues, 'that is because it is not in any degree a product of the reason, for its least elements were supplied to me by my sensibility, I perceived them first deep inside myself, without understanding them and had as much difficulty converting them into something intelligible as if they had been as alien to the world of the intellect – as what shall I say – a musical motif. You are thinking I imagine that this is over-subtle. But I assure you, on the contrary, that it is a reality. What we have not had to elucidate for ourselves, what was clear already (the ideas of logic for example), is not truly ours, we do not even know whether it is the real. It is a part of the "possible" that we select arbitrarily. Besides, you can tell that right away, you know, by the style.

'Style is not at all an embellishment as certain people think, it is not even a matter of technique, it is – like colour with painters – a quality of vision, the revelation of the private universe that each one of us can see and which others cannot see. The pleasure an artist affords us is to introduce us to one universe the more.'